Chronology of a Life Well Loved

Poems & Reflections

JOSEPH A. FATA

ISBN-13: 978-1974402076
ISBN-10: 197440207X

Library of Congress Control Number: 2017915576
CreateSpace Independent Publishing Platform
North Charleston, SC

Cover art by Joseph A. Fata
Cover design by CCA Graphics (Youngstown, Ohio)

First Printing: November, 2017
Printed and Bound in the United States of America
First Edition

Send inquiries to:
Richard Burke, Trustee
75 East Market Street
Akron, OH 44308

Dedicated to Brigid Kennedy

—Joseph A. Fata (July, 2016)

"Love is our true destiny.
We do not find the meaning of life
by ourselves alone—we find it with another."
—Thomas Merton

CONTENTS

FOREWORD

I am not a poet—far from it. But I greatly appreciate poetry, reading it often, praying it often. While pursuing my master's degree, I took several classes in poetry and through these discovered that good poetry shapes life. A good poem reaches deep within our being, awakening within us a variety of truths and calling us to rise and follow and discover more of who we are. Often such a poem brings to light a piece of us yet unknown urging us to claim this new part of ourselves. A poet is thus an artist who paints with words the canvas of life. Father Joseph Fata was such an artist.

I served six years with Joe at St. Joseph Parish in Mantua, OH. When I went for my initial interview with him for the position as pastoral minister, I expected the usual questions about my background and my credentials. This interview, far from those kinds of banal questions, lasted three hours because Joe, wanting to get a feel for my heart and my dreams, shared with me his heart and his dreams. As I drove back to Akron, I realized I had lived through an experience of grace. Joe had shared with me the heart of a pastor, of a shepherd who cares for God's people and makes himself available to God's people. The six years in ministry with Joe revealed this pastoral heart to me more and more deeply.

Above all else, Joe Fata was human in the best sense of that word. He was not perfect, and he knew it. He was honest and forthright about his vision and goals for the parish and its people. Both his heart and his intelligence moved him.

I am deeply honored to have been called on to write this Foreword, and I am sure that the reader of this book of poems will leave with both a sense of Joe's pastoral heart and of being touched by grace.

—Mary Ann Wiesemann-Mills, OP

PREFACE

A book's Preface is usually written by the author to give background information, often about the process of writing the book, the book's purpose or what inspired the writing. Joe Fata died 15 months before this book's publication and was unable to write its Preface, but the editorial committee decided that the story of how this book came to be is an important one to tell.

When Joe was sick, before we knew just how sick, I would visit in the evening to see that he had eaten, keep him company, and help him take his medications. He had stopped presiding at Mass, and he wasn't reading, writing or even listening to music. I was concerned that his spirits would worsen if he didn't resume doing something that he loved. He didn't think he could write creatively but said, "You know what I want to do? You and I sit here together every night. I'd like to read my poems to you. People have been after me to publish them, so maybe after I read a poem we can talk about what it means to me and whether it would have meaning to a wider audience."

And so we began. We read as many as he could, depending on how he felt. We didn't do them every night in the pre-hospice days, but we both looked forward to the ritual. Joe would ask "should we read some poems?" and he'd get his blue folder of poems, a red felt-tipped pen, the list of poems, and the next poem to read. Some poems didn't merit much conversation, but others were windows into his past. And we would decide yes, no or maybe; then Joe would mark the poem's fate. He checked off each poem on the list as we read it, and our progress pleased him. A few weeks after we began, he went into the hospital and from there to a hospice for a few nights before going home to the rectory for his last weeks.

We didn't read any poetry the first night in Hospice House, but the second night, very late, almost midnight, he asked me to get the folder. When he tried to read his voice was weak, and he had a reverberation in his ear, so he asked me to read to him instead.

The next night, his childhood best friend, Mike Basile, was going to stay overnight with him. So, after everyone else left, Joe told Mike that he and I were going to read poetry and Mike could sit in the room and listen or find something else to do if he wasn't interested. Of course, Mike stayed. That was the first time the reading was "public," and from that point we would begin reading late in the day but always before the last visitors had gone. Until the last poem was read, he never took a day off. Joe would read a poem if he felt his voice was strong enough, and two or three of us present would take turns reading others. Toward the end, Father Kevin Peters and Theresa Armile, who were there most nights to support or care for Joe, gained "preferred" status. If we knew they planned to be there, Joe and I would wait until they arrived to begin reading, marking, and crossing each poem off the master list, a precise routine that was an anchor in all the uncertainty.

By this time, the sessions became less about rating poems and more a shared experience of grace. At one point Kevin and I asked him if he'd like to start saying evening prayer as a small group, but he responded, rather matter-of-factly, "we are already doing that." The poetry reading had become our communal prayer. The poems were also a poignant review of his life, of intense and sometimes long-hidden moments of both joy and grief, all while surrounded by close friends and family. We cried our way through many of them, but we knew we were allowing Joe to better prepare for death and felt blessed to accompany him. We read the last poem with him two weeks before he died.

Joe's motivation for sharing his poems through this book was to offer his own experiences of grace and hubris, beauty and brokenness, so that others might find encouragement and consolation in similar experiences. Although he was unable to write this Preface himself, here are Joe's words from the Preface to his homily book, *From Mass to Mission*: "It is my prayer that any inspiration you gain from this book will be a trigger for a life of learning, loving and serving."

—Brigid Kennedy

ACKNOWLEDGMENTS

Joe had some clear hopes and ideas for this book. He envisioned a "poetry committee" that could handle any tasks necessary to bring the book to print. He wanted the committee members to have sat in on at least one of the nightly poetry reading sessions; to either be products of or at least mirror his theology and ecclesiology; and by his judgment, to have hearts and minds for poetry. The committee members he chose are all people who loved Joe and were loved and trusted *by* Joe: Theresa Armile, Lori Bagnola, Will Bagnola, Brigid Kennedy, Kevin Peters, Dick Ross and Susan Ross. For chapter introductions the committee tried to choose not only people who could speak to who Joe was during a place and time—the chronology or length of his life—but those who could represent the width and depth of his life as well: seminarian, brother, friend, mentor, social justice advocate, liturgist...We are grateful to Father Tom Dyer, Bob Roden, Will Bagnola, Mickey Fata, Pastor Michael Harrison, Theresa Armile and Donna Mertes for capturing moments of "a Life Well Loved" so well. Many thanks also to Sister Mary Ann Wiesemann for writing the Foreword, a tribute really, to Joe's "pastoral heart;" to Dick Ross for the Introduction; and to Brigid Kennedy for the Preface and for editing and preparing the manuscript. We are indebted to many people—too numerous to name—who supported and encouraged this project in ways big and small. Finally, to Joe's family: thank you for allowing us the opportunity to bring Joe's poems to a wider audience. It has been an honor and a labor of love.

INTRODUCTION

Poetry is a unique literary form that speaks from and to the deepest dimension of our humanity. Father Joseph Fata's poems began with his seminary training in the 1960s and ended the year before he died on August 1, 2016 after surviving cancer for 15 years. They provide a window into his spiritual perspective on the ordinary, whether about the pots and pans in his mother's kitchen or a solitary walk in the woods of land he loved. His poems reveal a profound grasp of the meaning and celebration of the liturgical cycle. He reflected through the years on the meaning of Easter, of betrayal, denial, injustice, death, and new life; of Christmas with poetic stories for which only Christmas can be the backdrop; and of surprising times in between. Life and death, love and loss, are found in both Gospel reflection and childhood anecdote, and ultimately, the Eucharistic tables of his family home and the church sanctuary are revealed as alike in their messages of welcome and abundance. In poetic form he captured his loneliness; his struggles as a celibate priest, despite or perhaps because of the magnanimous friendships he created; and his escapes to Lake Erie and to Italy, the land of his ancestors. These poems emerge from the landscape of five decades of disparate and momentous historical milestones without centering on these events themselves. His poetry is particular in place, time, and personal experience and yet offers universal truths: we recognize our own grief, joy, amazement and insecurity in his. This book represents a singular account of a life well lived and loved.

—Dick Ross

REMEMBERING JOE: "More Human"

Joe and I were friends for 46 years: we vacationed each summer at Lake Erie, attended annual Notre Dame Liturgy conferences, and shared regular Gourmet Club meals. We met in 1960 as we were entering St. Gregory Seminary in Cincinnati, with a rigorous academic, social and spiritual road ahead of us. We both did well in earlier schooling without much effort. That changed. We both had a basic homespun spirituality and a healthy social life. The seminary intended to mold each of us into the "perfect priest." Not unusual for the times. Not completely comfortable for all of us. But Joe was a determined student, and a man who sought style and grace, justice and resolution, simplicity and purpose. Joe found within himself beauty, intellect, creative order, and a drive for goodness, truth, peace, and friendship—gifts from God that made Joe an amazing person.

Thomas Merton said that we are called to be perfect as Christ is perfect: perfectly human, thus not less human but *more human*. Our sanctity, our holiness, is the capacity to be more sympathetic, more forgiving, more peaceful, more joyful, more appreciative of all that is right and good and just and beautiful in life. All who knew Father Joseph Fata know that his spirituality flowed from and was centered in the celebration of Liturgy. Every aspect had purpose and beauty, everyone had a significant role to play, and nothing was left to chance. The Worship of God is as human and holy an experience as could be assembled. And we all know he did it well, very well. But Joe Fata was not perfect and he might even (grudgingly) admit it! He saw the humor in life and in himself. He never missed an opportunity for wit or sarcasm. We all know many funny stories about Joe: his reaction to the poor waitress who said to him, "Penne or ziti, what does it matter? Pasta is pasta." Or the young woman who went to the store and returned with cool whip instead of whipping cream. And who will forget the theatrics over his fear of needles?

I invite you to enjoy what follows because it comes from the mind, heart and soul of a good man, an outstanding priest, a worthy yet not perfect child of God. And a great friend of many, many!

—Father Thomas Dyer

CHAPTER ONE
EARLY YEARS & SEMINARY DAYS (1960-1967)

NEEDLE AND THREAD

I am afraid of what I might be.
The Thread that sustains me
is so thin.
The thinness is my own doing.
And less than thin,
the Thread with its
needle has pierced
that part of me
which is weakest,
    Love.
But God,
if you strengthen the Thread
I will increase the Love
    —not alone, of course.
But together
we will bind the world
and bind it
and bind it again
until it is all lost
in the wonder of
the Thread.

WINDY BOY

Once, long time ago,
so long I'm not sure when,
a windy boy
was blown into the ark of perfection
I was building for myself.
I don't know where he came from
but his small eyes were wide with excitement
he could not control.
And I could tell
he had been nourished at the roots
of a Great Oak.
And I,
I had fed mostly on other stuff.
He knows what it's like
to stand on a hill
with weeds waist high
and to barely see at the bottom
a creek full of minnows and crayfish and pollywogs.
He moved very silently
and no doubt, Someone Else
saw him first.
But when I saw him
standing on the edge of where I was living,
his blue jeans were rolled up to his knees
and his feet were wet
and he had a prize for me.
Huckleberry Finn—Windy Boy.

On the sandpaper floor of my ark
he made wet footprints
(more than necessary),
because of his dancing.
Dumb David! (Who danced before Yahweh)
I dance too, but not like that!
And just when it seemed like those flashing feet
would soon be dry
he'd race off to some hidden, whispering, forever-flowing stream
springing from some strange, exciting, wind-blown oasis.
Rebirth. Everyday. With the Sun.

Silently
he boasted of things
too beautiful to be real,
too real to be precious,
too precious to be repeated by me.
As silently as the Windy Boy speaks,
so silently must I understand.
Silently
like the Moving ancient Waters
that engulf our tired feet
even when we don't know it.
Windy Boy
Windy Boy
Windy Boy.
My shoes are off.

A PROMISE

Sometimes
we meet someone
and we miss the
chance to say
"I love you."
And it never comes again
—the chance.
But that someone has made
an impression.
And that someone doesn't know it.
And we don't tell.
The walls of our own
insecurity
and the tears of our own
discontent
won't let us tell.
But I've made myself
a promise.
I'm going to start
telling...
It will be hard at first.
People might not
understand.
But I'm going to be brave.
I'll do it.

YOU KNOW HOW DREAMS ARE

A long time ago
or maybe yesterday
    —I can't say for sure
    'cause dreams have
    no time—
it rained.
And I listened
to the rain for a long time too.
I memorized what it
sounded like
    —just in case
    I never
    hear it again.
Then I went to
the window.
I watched the
little beads of water
on the other side
where I couldn't touch them.
Then I closed my eyes
for a second.
When I opened them again
each bead of water
was a stepping stone
and the window was me
    (you know how dreams are)
and I stood in the first stone
ready to tip-toe
across myself
when a beautiful Spanish girl
took my hand.
She didn't talk.
She hummed a song.
Somehow she told me secrets.
She told me not to fall
and that love and joy
and sorrows and tears
have no bounds.

She told me
that the walls of confusion
are paper thin
and are easily toppled
and that somewhere
flowers bloom year 'round
and that the right people
understand when
I act on impulse
even if they number
only one or two.
She promised
to answer all my questions
sometime...
Sometime is a magic word
because then
I woke up.
I felt like a bright, shiny stone
at the bottom of a
clear creek.
But my dream was gone.
There was nothing left...
Nothing but
the rain
the window
and me,
the beads of water
and the stepping stones,
the Spanish girl
and the messages she wrote
across my brain
and in my heart.
Is that confusing?
Well, you know how dreams are.

SO MANY PEOPLE (Winter, 1964)

My eyes are burned.
I should blink
but I don't.
I keep waiting for someone
to look,
for people to look.
People!
That sounds like Barbra Streisand.
I think she's people,
but maybe not.
Anyway,
I keep waiting for people
to look.
There are so many people
here.
But they're not really people.
I don't even know
if they're really here.
And they look
but not really.
If they would look
they'd see me
ready to burst
like an over-ripe pomegranate.
I see some of them
ready to burst
like pomegranates.
They don't even know it
themselves.
And I can't tell them.
They wouldn't listen.

So
I go to my room,
my fallout shelter...
        I got that from
        Thomas Merton.
        He's really people.

I guess I'm all
idols like
Thomas Merton
and
Joan Baez
and
John Kennedy
and
John XXIII
and
Francie Kelly.
      (She writes like this.)
Anyway...
I go to my room
and I go to my
window
and I look in.
You might say
"out."
But I say
"in"
because I think
the people "out there"
are really "in"
and I'm "out"
even though I'm
in here.
So I look in
at them
and I see more
pomegranates.
Really ripe
and ready to burst.
If only someone
would help them
burst.
But I can't
because they're in
and I'm out.
And besides,
the stripes on my window
say "no."

So they're almost bursting
in there where I'm not
and they're almost bursting
out here
where I am.
But the people in there
can't hear me
and the people out here
won't listen.
So we all sit,
out here
and in there
ready to burst
but we never will.
We'll never burst because we
don't
help each other.
And so we'll never be
people really.
Until we burst.
But we don't know how.
     I think
     secrets
     are the answer
     but I'm not sure.

MEDITATION (1964)

My fellows and I walk
quietly as feathers.
We can only hear each other's silence.
Meditation.
Suddenly, we are jarred from our sleep.
There in the sky,
like the biblical "King robed in splendor,"
the Sun lingers,
for one last look at his earthly court.
Around him are colors only
God has on his palette:
a flaming mixture of dazzling hues
purples and golds and pinks and blues,
shades that Picasso never knew.
A riot of color,
proof of God's greatness.
But such wonder cannot last,
and as we watch the golden sphere
sinks,
sinks,
sinks,
like a giant ship,
into the ocean of its own beauty.
We go back to our meditations,
small meditations.

WHAT IS THERE?

What is there
beneath the selfish and generous
the rough and smooth?
Christ. Christ.
That's what I would hope.
The surge of power
that I don't understand
is like a wave that
smashes itself to death
on a rock
that never moves or feels
but gradually
only gradually
bears the mark
of the ocean
that embraces it.

COMMUNITY ROOM (1964)

When I get restless
it's like a big wind
whipping through me.
As it whirls around
it scoops up objects
        —odds and ends—
lying around on the floor
of my brain.
It smacks them
against the inside
of my skull
so that each little object
        —they seem bigger now—
shatters into
a thousand question marks.
You know,
I could never even begin
to pick them up alone.
And that's when
my restlessness shows
        when I start moving.
It's kind of embarrassing.

If I am lucky
I find someone.
But I can't tell you
what happens
because it never happens
the same way twice.
There is no experience
like exchanging glances
with Jesus.
    (Looking beyond the face
    you don't even like.)
I'm not too good at it.
But it's warm,
it makes restlessness
go away.
You can look
into a face or eyes
and see
rain and failure,
sunshine and smiles,
tears and smashed hopes,
faith and joy,
and sometimes even
loving back.
All by exchanging glances
with Jesus.
It's not really Jesus,
but really, it is.

Maybe these thoughts
sound like
too much imagination
but that doesn't make them
less real.
The sweeping up of question marks
makes it real.
My stumbling proves it's real.
My bungling
over-stated
over-emotional
never-ending
stumbling
proves it's real.

I WISH (January, 1965)

If I could only
stand still
for a minute.
But I can't.
I have to keep
looking.
I wish I knew for sure
what I am looking for.
I wish I knew.
Sometimes
I go down to that "cupboard."
On the way
I have a pretty good idea
of what I am looking for
or who. Whom?
Anyway,
I have a pretty good
idea.
But then I get there
and forget.
Or maybe I don't forget.
Maybe I just change my mind.
There they all are,
each one on his own
little shelf.
I know the person
I'm looking for is there.
I even see him.
    (Sometimes it's them.)
But when I see him,
or them,
I pretend I wasn't really
looking for anyone
at all.
Least of all him
or them.
So I don't talk.
After all,
I wouldn't want
it to seem
like I depend
on anyone else.

I'm proud.
I'm self-centered.
Or at least it seems that way.
I wish I didn't
pretend.
I wish I could
go up to him
or them
and say,
"Hey you,
I was just looking for you."
Or maybe,
"I'm glad I found
you here."
But I never do.
Neither does anyone else.
But that's no excuse.
Someone
has to start it,
start tearing down
the shelves, I mean.
It might as well be
me.
I'll do it.
I guess I should practice.
"Hey you,
I was just looking
for you."
"Hey you,
I was just looking..."

I'll do it.
(I've said that before.)
And I'll borrow a line
from a friend of mine.
"Esther,
would it embarrass you
if I said
I love you?"

MAYBE (Spring, 1965)

I wish there were some way
to be more clear.
Some of the things I try
to say to people come out
all thick and fuzzy.
It just seems that nobody understands me.
Now, I don't mean that in the sense of
"Boo hoo, nobody understands me."
What I mean is
        —well it just seems that
my thoughts aren't clear to people.
Sometimes my words only make
little walls that
people can't see over.
Sometimes I think that
it might be better
if I would just keep quiet
and let people "feel" what I'm thinking.
I guess I'm just a lot of emotion
and too little brains.
That also makes me too frisky.
People don't like "frisky."
They don't like it when
I bust myself in to where they are
        —in their heads—
and I can't blame them.
I try to understand how they feel.
It's hard for me.
I don't think I'm that different,
yet, I've been looking
and I really can't find
anyone like me.
Maybe I'm too much
inside myself,
you know, too close to home.
Maybe someone can tell me,
"Look, you're like this or that
or like that one over there."
It's easy for me
to look at someone else and say
what's wrong with him in my book.

Maybe if I could find someone
like me I could watch him
and find out about me.
Someone said
we can't change our personalities.
Well, I don't want to do that,
at least I don't think so.
I like myself too much.
(That could be the problem!)
Still, there are things
I could change, I think.
Everyone could.
Someone else told me that
when he first met me
he thought I needed a friend.
My pride was hurt.
I mean, we all need friends
and I do have friends,
loyal ones too
        —more than me.
And most of the time
I don't give them
enough credit or attention.
But what I'm getting
around to saying is:
I just wish these friends
would point things out to me
once in a while.
Maybe they think I would feel bad and cry
        —or something.
Maybe I would.

I'M GLAD I FOUND OUT (November, 1965)

I'm glad I found out.
Every experience means so much
to me.
And I used to say,
"I wish I could be less sensitive."
But now I don't.
I'm glad.
I want every experience (encounter)
to really matter.
A lot of people will go
tramping through
my life.
I hope they leave big
Footprints.
Sometimes it will hurt.
      —footprints, I mean.
But that doesn't matter
'cause that's how
I grow.
I guess I need the caresses too.
No doubt
they give me confidence,
at least for the moment.
But the footprints that hurt
are the ones that really count,
the footprints that leave
big scars
all over my insides.
Love without scars
isn't worth it
      —He knew that—
and now I know it.
I'm glad I found out.
Just think,
I could have lived my whole life
hiding on the edge of my world.
I would have ended up without
one footprint on me.
I wouldn't have left any either.
That'd be sad.
I'm glad I found out.

THAT'S GROWING (November, 1965)

"The sky's changing color
I must go where it's quiet."*

Growing sure is funny,
and every day
I become more of age.
You know
growing is lots of things.
Mostly it's those
Footprints.
But it's other things too.

I grew the last two weeks
like I never thought I could.
(I know people come and go
in our lives.)
And I said
"yes"
to it.
I knew my insides would end up
curdled.
But I said
"yes"
anyway.
See,
I really didn't have
a "right"
to what I had
and wanted to keep.
It took lots of growing
to realize this.
So I gave it back.
Really, it was taken,
but I feel like I gave it back
because I agreed,
and I grew.
It was sad, footprint
type growing.
But I grew.
Now I'm making room
for other growing.

I found out that
growing
is smiling back at someone
who has been smiling
at you for a long time.
But when you are so busy
with distractions
you never notice.
      Don't resent the distractions.
      After all, it is growing.
And besides
it's such a great smile.
I'm glad I looked
before it was turned off.
I wonder just how many
smiles
there are that I haven't noticed.
I'll have to be on the
lookout.
Besides
I need something to
fill up the hole
where the distraction was.
And I'm selfish enough
to use smiles.
But, it's really not selfish
because I'm going to smile back.
I mean really smile back.
Not just surface smiling
but a smile from the soul.

But that doesn't mean
I won't cry sometimes, does it?
But that's alright.
That's growing.

(*from "Farewell, Angelina" by Bob Dylan)

A REFLECTION ON RACE (March, 1966)

Where is Rosalia?
Rosalia Cross.
She has gone,
she has fled
through the wild nights of clover.
The willow weeps louder now.
All your pages are empty.
And where is Rosalia?
Rosalia Cross.
For one hundred years
she had crawled, she had begged.
When her head was split open
all her thoughts flowed so easy.
You all turned in horror.
You would not believe it.
And where is Rosalia?
Rosalia Cross.
We are friends
we are foes,
lovers and leavers.
She is kind, she is brutal.
Her absence is welcome.
Do we stand secure now?
Is there none to condemn us?
Yes.
Where is Rosalia?
Rosalia Cross.

THE RUDEST AWAKENING (November, 1966)

Wonder-working, dancing, singing Jesus
love me for my good intentions.

The rude awakening of failure
comes with lyrics like
"Daddy you been on my mind..."
And rejection is shot
into the stomach
like an arrow.
Then it lies there
like a 12-pound rock.
While all of me
cries out
"please don't go."
But it does go
and failure is real
just like love,
just like love
that lives beyond
the failure.
You know
the scar of a lay-awake-night
is deep
and is never filled in.

The subsequent exchange is not enough
and whets the soul's appetite
for deeper touches.
But God gives strength
　　—the strength to smile
　　and watch from a
　　respectful distance—
while we live
a prayer for
growth
and dream the idealist's dream
for a happy ending.

But on some
Mondays, Wednesdays and Fridays
I know it's an
unlikely dream.

21

So I close my eyes
to keep a face out
and a tear in
and nobody knows
except maybe a
mysterious one or two.

But between tears
the idealist lives
and smiles and grows
and does
what he hopes is right
and good
for the self
for the other
(though I'm not sure).
And the flame of the
I-Thou
dances small
but hopefully
waiting
to become a
full blown fire
that will consume
and be consumed
in a happy ending.

But maybe happy endings
are for movies only.
Maybe it will never come
because I've looked
in the wrong places.
But I've been
captured
and can't think otherwise,
so that my smiling, crying
existence whirls me
madly,
on orange wings
through lifetimes
of hopelessness and love.

What makes me secure
is at once disarming.
It seems the only acceptable excuse
is a note from Home.
And the only excuse I have
is me.

But "me" is not enough.
And that is the rudest awakening
of all.

THE PRISON GUARD AT ROUEN (1966)

See the girl in that cell?
She's Joan of Arc, I know her well.
She's from my village—Domrémy.
I don't think she remembers me.
She used to watch her father's sheep.
You could tell her thoughts were dark and deep.
She was, of all, the strangest one.
I was always sure she'd be a nun.
At those times when the children would play,
She'd sneak off alone to pray.
As she grew the solitude increased.
I mentioned it once to the parish priest.
He said to wait, her time would come.
Little did I know, I'd be the one.

THE KEEPING BAG (1967)

Now and then,
I sweep up my thoughts.
They're like shavings
that clutter the floor
of an old carpenter's shop.
Tenderly
I brush the curly creatures
(everything is alive you know)
onto a small wooden dustpan,
not unaware, I mix
shavings and splinters.
For the splinters are dreams
fulfilled,
unfulfilled,
to be fulfilled.
And they hold my thoughts
together
sometimes.
Quickly I stuff everything
into my Keeping Bag.
    Keeping Bags are for
    things like
    thoughts and dreams.
    They are strong enough
    to last forever
    and small enough
    to be carried unseen.
I draw the strings
around the top,
secure,
until one of those
special days comes by
when,
encouraged by
the bits of sun I've captured,
and the Keeping Bag
held close to my
cooling chest,
I'm refired to truth.

The strings go slack,
almost miraculously,
and the precious contents
of my Keeping Bag
go spiraling out,
wildly but with dignity.
But they always come back
—the contents—
because you can never lose
what was once in a
Keeping Bag.
They always come back
and wait patiently
for the next
special spiraling day.
More often than not,
it's a long wait.
But things have a way
of staying fresh in a
Keeping Bag.
Besides,
if something is worth anything
it's worth waiting for.
And everyone knows
how much
special spiraling days
are worth.

REMEMBERING JOE: "The Word"

"The Word was made flesh and dwelt amongst us." (John 1:14)

As music director at Our Lady of Peace, I served with Father Fata in a time of graceful fluidity within the Church. Since we were both a bit strong-willed, our initial relationship was somewhat confrontational. However, we became friendly collaborators on a single issue: our devotion to liturgical prayer. We worked with a group of visionaries to ensure that all aspects of celebrations were as inspirational as possible. No aspect of Mass was left to chance: Scripture, homily, Eucharist, music and environment.

Words can create a beautiful picture, assist in better understanding, mend or wound a heart. Father Fata was fascinated by words and had a gift for weaving words into beautiful and meaningful fabric. He wrote, "My life is peppered with the Word/seasoned with the Word/sustained by the Word....The Word/taking my life, giving me life." At Mass, we were not only fed by the Bread of Life, but also nourished by Joe's inspiring homilies. His messages made The Word dwell in our hearts and stirred us to action.

Just as those of us who share in the Bread of Life will never die, Joe Fata's words live on and continue to nurture our lives.

—Bob Roden

CHAPTER TWO
OUR LADY OF PEACE, CANTON (1974-1981)

EASTER FOR A CHURCH IN GROWING PAIN (1974)

How easily Easter passes
while we
    —supposedly shot through
    with new life—
get on with the business of dying.
With half-hearted Alleluias
we welcome the Risen Lord
and give lazy lip service
to St. Augustine's claim that
"We are Easter people…"
When in fact, we would rather
curb our spirits
than allow our souls to soar
in Easter exaltation.
We may deny it
but practice proves the point.
Living in Lenten ruins
is more in keeping
with our warped
sense of celebration.
Forty days of preparation.
    One day of celebration.
        A lifetime of denial
        and false creeds
        not living what we say
        we believe.
Where are the believers
who wait anxiously in upper rooms
for the breath of the Spirit?

Where are the disciples
recognizing him
in the breaking of the bread?
Where are the women
running
out of breath
astonished
yet hopeful?
I have trouble seeing.
Upper rooms have been traded
for patios and pools and cabin cruisers
where we wait,
not for the Spirit
but for the next bowl of potato chips
and mixed drink
and proclaim the coming of nothing.

And disciples recognizing him
in the breaking of the bread
have been replaced by robot Christians
who peer into mirrors and see nothing
because they have exchanged
broken bread for broken promises
and turned their backs
on the only one who can pick up the pieces.
And instead of women
running
out of breath
astonished
yet hopeful
we can see
at the doors of our churches
like at a tomb's entrance
late-comers and early-leavers
leaning
bored and empty
soul-less
against vestibule walls
claiming (about liturgy)
"I don't get anything out of it"
condemning themselves
before the Christ
who looks at them disappointed and says:
"Neither do I."

And yet
in spite of, or maybe
because of
our preoccupation
with sin and suicide
Christ persistently
overturns the mixing bowl
of frustration and anger.
Snowstorms inevitably turn to sunshine
    —even if we do draw the drapes
    and run for cover.
And the dingy, crust-covered earth
shoots daffodils defiantly at us
while we gas up the power mowers
of our soul-lessness
and bounce rough-shod
over the soggy grass.

It is an eternal war.
    Rejection and reconciliation.
    Alienation and acceptance.
And the only encouragement
is the fact that we can't win.
Christ,
Risen and new
not just for Easter
but for everyday
won't let us win.
Hallelujah!
Just when we, Thomas-like
have begun doubting God
and one another
and ourselves
Christ cuts through
the rock of our tomb
and says hopefully:
"Peace be with you."
And sensing our disbelief
knowing our desire for death
seeing our struggle
feeling our last feeble attempt
to shut him out
clinches it
and repeats himself.

His word becomes an echo
penetrating finally and forever
into the cotton-filled ears
of mediocre men and women.
He says forever and again:
"Peace be with you."
"Peace be with you."

CHAIN OF HEARTS

Letting love loose
into a life
is a risk
not taken with vapid words
or empty gestures.
No,
it requires
an immeasurable wealth
that lavishly overflows
with simplicity and strength
becoming a gentle torrent
that will not be turned
from its course
—not be dried in the desert
of selfishness or vanity.

We are secured then
and held together
not by a single
isolated love
but rather
by a chain of hearts
that links us to the past
rings-us-round
lifts us up
and flies us into tomorrow.

UNCLE ORESTE (1977)

"Eh, Little Black Sambo"
    —in broken English
    stuttering, stammering.
And a box full of army hats.
Lots of memories going
round and round.
I remember at least a little.
    A red Dodge
    and a ride on Sunday
    for frozen custard.
    Pomegranates and prickly pears
    and Brandy Alexanders
    in little silver chalices
    (in a little apartment).
    I was little too.
    And don't forget
    fifty cents
    for "cleaning the kitchen."
    He was rich then I thought.

And then
Christmas
New Year's
Palm Sunday
Easter
Thanksgiving
    —always late for dinner
    with a silly grin
    to cut the tension.
    It worked every time.
    A hot little temper too
    like a flash.

Gardens, flowers, colored stones and bricks,
all in neat arrangement.
A feeble attempt
if it were only done
to make life orderly.
But no!
Some inner drive instead.
Who knows why?

And don't forget the tears
    —on every occasion.
More so later.
Memories
so strange...big gaps
yet seeming to cover every single day.

Memories
that linger
like the song of
the summer birds
in the heart's ear
when winter comes
and they pack up
their instruments
and fly away.

WINDSONG (1980)

In the leaves there is a windsong
In the clouds there is a radiance
In the wildflower there is a sunburst
In the good earth there is love
    In my life there is room for you
    In my thoughts there is a place for you
    In my dreams there are shades of you
    In my heart, signs of love
        And so I ask you to see
        If in your life there is room for me
        If in your dreams there is a place for me
        In your heart, is there any love
In the meadow there is a dewshower
On the bird's wing there is freedom
In the summer rain there is a rainbow
In the sunshine there is love
    Don't you see you're my windsong
    You're my radiance, you're my sunburst
    Don't you see you're my love
        Don't you see you're my dewshower
        You're my freedom
        You're my rainbow
        Don't you see you're my love...

A PREFACE FOR YOU (1980)

Reaching for words
insensitive to the vulnerability
of caring too much
or knowing too little
I offer you these thoughts:
    love and friendship.

And if it is true
that I am "favored everyday"
because I give
"the heart's great gift"
then I give it
to you
for the sun-streaked colors
that melt into the eyes of my mornings.

The high wire is stretched taut
across the canyon of life.
We rip and tear
at the clouds
searching for reasons
    sunshine
    and who knows what.

And if my words could sail
on billowed wings
they'd vault the sky.
And if my heart could carry sound
it would tell of all the love it's found.
If my hands could fashion words like clay
I would carve a monument to say:
    A skyful of love
    falls into our lives
    each day.

GOD IS SO FULL OF SURPRISES (Epiphany, 1980)

Is God so full of surprises
or are we so shortsighted and narrow?
Or maybe a little of both.
It seems God never reveals himself
in ways we would expect
or be comfortable with.

How can God reveal himself
in the solitude of monasticism and
in the fierceness of Islam and
in the pain of sickness and
in the tragedy of death and
in the exuberance of life?
But reveal himself he does.
And this revelation,
this manifestation,
this epiphany
comes at the end of the search,
our search for God,
God's search for us.

And in our prejudices
where we see entire countries as villainous
　　—as if their skies were not blue—
where we see entire races as unreliable
　　—as if their blood were not red—
where we see entire cultures as underdeveloped
　　—as if their hearts had no longing—
in these prejudices
we must encounter
epiphany
with Magi, strange men,
astrologers,
foreigners,
plodding along,
following the light in their sky,
the light in their hearts.
Searching, open, hoping,
leaving behind those "pleasure domes,"
the comfort of home.
Leaving behind the things that men crave.
Leaving behind sin and self.

Searching, following, fumbling
with a foolish star
skating across the icy cold winter sky.

How could God reveal himself to these men?
How could God reveal himself in the arms
of a plain, young country girl,
in the ordinary cry of a Jewish baby?
But reveal himself he did.
And they knew something
       —those strange men, those astrologers, those star-gazers.
They didn't know it all.
They only scratched the surface of mystery.
But they knew something.
And they brought gold—he was a king!
And frankincense—how else do you worship God?
And myrrh—how else do you prepare for death?
Yes, they knew something.
So they went,
these astrologers, these stargazers, these foreigners,
plodding along
following the light in their sky,
the light in their hearts.

How unlike other kings
and presidents
and dictators
and rulers
who foster our fear,
promote our prejudice,
bolster our bias.
Directors of darkness
who have never seen a star
in their own sky or in another's.

Yes, God is so full of surprises.
His light shines in strange places
where babies are born
and old men die,
where shepherds and stargazers
have the presence of mind to look up.
God is so full of surprises.
And God's Epiphanies
wait for no king's approval.

THIS IS WHY WE WAIT (Easter, 1980)

Waiting
with candles and hearts burning,
wide-eyed with wonder,
wondering if the rumor will be true,
wanting to trade empty hearts for an empty tomb,
wanting those hearts to be overflowing with light and life,
wishing more than daffodils into bloom this Spring.

Here we sit,
waiting,
so many islands
wanting to come together
even if we don't know it,
clutching our own light,
hoping someone will notice our little flicker of brightness.
And yet knowing, deep down, that when
the life-spirit blows through
only one light can remain.
One bright light.
The Easter Light.
The Easter Life.
The Christ Light
in which we all share.
No more can we be satisfied
with individual flickers,
wanting all kinds of things
and being satisfied with none of them.
We really long to be drawn into
that one flame.

And so we wait.
Waiting is difficult.
Faith makes it bearable.
Hope makes it exciting.
Love makes it a joy.
We wait,
listening to the words that
gave our Jewish ancestors hope.

And yet possessing a deeper dimension,
we stand with one eye on the cross
and the other on the tomb,
feeling caught in the middle,
knowing the story can't end this way.
Hot on the heels of the cross
are infinite Alleluias
waiting for their chance,
waiting for their time,
waiting for the Word, the Word.
And when the Word is finally
spoken, reborn, lived,
then all heaven will break loose (for a change)
and we remember,
re-sing the angels' songs.
The tombs we have
sealed up with our sinfulness
break open.
And as the angel rolls away the stone,
we see the loving face
that disintegrates
the rocks in our heads and in our hearts.
We will be fertile ground once more.
Room for growing.
Finally and forever there is life.
This is why we wait.
When all is said and sung,
we wait for nothing less than
Light and Life forever.

ALLELUIAS OF A DIFFERENT SORT (Easter, 1981)

The fire dances
self-consciously at first
catching its breath
flaming into brightness
secured at last
and sure of its place
while we stand
wax and wick
flesh and blood
ignited by flame and faith.

> We have remembered again
> the place in the woods
> the words
> the dance
> and how to light the fire.

The fire watches us
burning truth into our lives
and as I stare back
flickering
eye to eye
I can see the images of Easter
once cornered into my heart
now somersaulting out of hiding
tumbling like jelly beans from a jar.
My life is the spinning wheels
of the chartered bus
that drives me into Holy Weeks past.
My memory is as vivid
as the smell of anise
in my mother's Easter kitchen
when her hands were strong
and she baked the bread
that was another sacrament
with a magic all its own...
Mounds of dough
kneaded, oiled, panned and blessed.

Then baked and prepared
for the ritual exchanges
between family and friends
coming to my father's house
with alleluias of a different sort
arms brimming over
weighed down
with wine and cakes
bright baskets
chocolate eggs
symbols that even now seem appropriate
to victims of adulthood.
Tapestried into my mind:
     cheese pie and lamb
     Gregorian chant and Tenebrae
     hours of adoration
     and white processions to special places
     veiled and ablaze.
All the realities
whisk like a shuttle
across the weaver's loom
formed and patterned
into the colors of my life.
And today we
     fired, worded, woven into the fabric
     of one another's lives
wait for the sparkling water
fountained over our heads
flooding our dryness
and floating the darkness away
as the Risen Son of God
warm and living
moves gently into
our cold lives
like the Rising Sun of morning
thick and amber bright
pouring and oozing in
through our windows
honeyed into our eyes
sweetening and enlivening
the cold, left-over memory
of dull winter hearts.

O speak that word to me again.
    Shout it.
    Whisper it.
    Tender it.
    Speak it into life.
    Touch me so I will know I live.

In the beginning God created...
And He never stopped.

Now we
fragile vessels
ride that stream of consciousness
right up to Our Father's Table
where another Easter Bread
is kneaded into a loaf that
consumes us
creates us
fashions us into a people
and loves us into being once again.

OUR LADY OF PEACE FAREWELL (June 29, 1981)

There were nights
when I wished myself to sleep
wanting to capture and then release words
like Robert Frost or Dylan Thomas.
And then one day it happened.
The cork popped and the words
champagned onto the page.
The book,
bound and cased before,
was cracked now
and the words fluttered and flew
like summer birds
into the skies of the people I love,
like seeds scattering
when the envelope is ripped open,
like seeds falling
onto the soil of the hearts
of the people who love me.

I know
we all have words wintered
in our brains
waiting for a summer heart
to sunshine them into bloom.

Love is ushered or coaxed or rushed
out of my heart,
unpacked
like the big suitcase
at vacation's end.
In the unpacking
the poured out, empty heart
becomes a home
where hospitality is hung
and there is space for everyone.

And my journey,
the inevitable road
is not like the overgrown
trails and towpaths
through the wooded refuge of my life
but more clear-cut and lined,
macadamed and steamrolled before me
inviting me
calling me
urging me.
And if looking back,
        to see the footprints
        pressed into where I've been,
if looking back is difficult or painful
it is a mirroring
a remembering
of the footprints of those
who walk with me.

And as I move along
I gather up
like seashells
the people poured into the stream
like Easter Water
cascading and spraying
over the rocks that birth flowers
and promise life.
I bundle them up
into the knapsack of my heart
        the flowers and the people
and take them with me
        poured, sparkled
        into the flagon of happiness
        slung over my shoulder.

To be prophet or poet or visionary
is too much
and so I push my little car
now through tears
now through laughter
always through the seasons
each one sparking a special excitement.

Summer—warmed into brightness
Fall—paintbrushed across the sky
Winter—snowed over the hills
Spring—blossomed through the soil.

My life is like the seasons
full and overwhelming
chocolate-sundaed into my bowl,
mounded and heaped to overflowing.
My life is peppered with the Word
    seasoned with the Word
    sustained by the Word.
The Word   —winepressed into my heart
           —flashed into my eyes
           —cupped into my ears
           —breathed into my mouth.
The Word   —filling every space
           —looking to me to speak it into sound.
The Word   —taking my life, giving me life.
The Word   —with us always
           —until the end of the world.
And then some.

REMEMBERING JOE: "Just Up the Hill"

Joe Fata was a great pastor and a thought-provoking preacher. He had the knack of drawing from people the gifts that each could contribute to the parish to help build up the Body of Christ. I first met Joe in July 1983, when I was assigned an internship at St. Joe's, Mantua. My life, my ministry, would never be the same. Among so many shared experiences, one stands out: our trip to Savuto, the village where his father, Natale, was born and where Joe's aunts and cousins were still living.

Joe and I got off the train from Sicily that September morning in Amantea, Calabria, in search of Savuto. We had no idea where Savuto was. As it turned out, it was far enough away that we had to backtrack south by train, to Campora San Giovanni, where we checked into a hotel and were told that Savuto was "just up the hill." We called the only phone in Savuto, in its only bar, and were again told to go "just up the hill," which of course translated into a thirty-minute car ride.

We were let out at the square, really nothing more than the end of the road, went into the bar, and asked for his aunt, Cristina. The barista called out to a younger woman in a doorway in the alley. She was Cristina's daughter Maria, who cried as we explained who we were and led us up another alley to her parents' house: a small, poor place with a million-dollar view from the kitchen window. Cristina was confused at first, but then pulled out Joe's ordination picture in recognition. When Joe's aunt Carmella arrived, she cried, and then kept looking and smiling at Joe. Carmella was more jovial, Cristina more somber. Joe would later say that looking into Cristina's face was like looking into the face of his father.

At the time, Joe wrote, "I can't describe my feelings when we got there. It was like going to a place, and feeling I had seen it in a dream....Nothing looked strange or new to me! It was a little like going someplace I had seen pictures of, yet I never have. The village is beautiful in an artistic and ancient kind of way...like what I would expect in the Holy Land or some biblical movie."

—Will Bagnola

CHAPTER THREE
ST JOSEPH, MANTUA & SAVUTO (1981-1988)

POETRY AND PROMISE (Villa Maria Retreat, 1981)
Ex. 12:37-42, Mt. 12:14-21

Like the Israelites of old
we too are a crowd of mixed ancestry
shaped
(who knows how)
into a people of faith,
a worshipping community.
We too keep vigils and remember.
We are the bruised reeds,
bending and bowing,
the smoldering wicks,
brittle and ashen.
Now healed.
Now set ablaze.

We GATHER
on the cutting edge of our existence
and discover our need.
We PROCLAIM
the Word
into the chasm of our lives
and the questions
canyoned in our history
are echoed back at us.

We BREAK BREAD
over the pottery of our creviced souls
and the answer
baked into our Tradition
is crumbled into our hands.
We POUR WINE
from the flagon of our discontent
and peace,
always a touch away,
cascades into our dry hearts.

Who dares touch this reality?
Who could plumb the depths mysteried into our souls?

We search for
poetry and promise.
We reach for
sign, symbol and hope.

Looking in all the other places first...
finding nothing or less...
we come back to
Water and Word
Bread and Wine
common things,
and discover who we are.

CHANGE OF SEASON (September, 1981)

The year steals
into golden colors
and the crisp clear staccato notes
come blasting from
the Horn of Autumn.

My window is a picture frame
embracing a canvas
of then and now
reality and memory mingling excitedly
triggered by the image
of an old teacher
staggering across the shiny floor
in front of the occupied runnered desks
giving flesh to an old poem:
      "Autumn in her scarlet cloak
      comes tumbling down the hill."

The sumac is first
like the talk show host
announcing coming attractions
while everyone tunes in
for a clearer picture.

Rickety road-side stands
pop up like happy mushrooms
mounded with
pumpkins, peppers and squash
sure signs that the demise of summer
is irreversible and beyond resuscitation.

Yellow school busses
carrying an ambivalent cargo
to secret places in the mind
roll over the ice cream vendor's truck
leaving the treats of summer
in the nooks and crannies
of childhood memory.

High school bands
scramble unsuccessfully
for notes that flutter elusively
through the chilly air
and settle
inevitably
beyond reach.

Clear cold evenings appear
out of darkness
shrouded in frost
that penetrates
the old bones of big houses
making them
creak and shift in the night
groping for a comfortable position
to survive the winter.

The Canada geese
all gaggled and grouped
honking the season
slide their way
through the grey sky
obviously on a pressing mission
to glassy coves
and lazy lakes.

Fireplaces and old stoves
come alive again
rekindled like old friendships
crackling and sparking
brightened with flames
hungrily attacking the cold air
like children lapping at popsicles.

The smell of those special breads and cakes
mingling with the unmistakable pungency
of tomatoes, peppers and pickles
being bottled and stored
remind us that there really was a summer
and it will appear again
as surely as the empty mason jars.

And finally
we ourselves reflect
the tide of time and change of season
as we emerge
with shoulders sweatered
and heads capped
as if to keep in our minds
the thoughts of warm cider
and deep rich wine
while the blood in our veins
makes the adjustment
and we carry in our arms
like logs for the fire
hopes and dreams
to warm us through the winter.

THESE DREAMS OF MINE (Valentine's Day, 1982)

And if
like Meštrović or Michelangelo
I could sculpt,
I would scoop up
words
and shape them,
breathing life into them,
making them wax and wane
like sun and moon,
blowing them up like bright balloons,
letting them burst and confetti in my mind,
setting them to float in the currents
like great armadas conquering the seas,
whetting them to bite like tangy peppercorns,
sending them to soar like flashing condors,
pushing them to plummet like supple divers
arcing and splaying in my thoughts,
plunging into pages that would be leafed
only to cascade like a giant autumn oak
on the lives of those whose eyes
would devour and consume them
making them part of their own experience.

These dreams of mine
are like the choreography on a country clothesline
where overalls jump and dance
wild in the wind
seemingly with life of their own.

So my dreams about words and life
        —even if they never come true—
are their own reason for being
just like love not always expressed
but known by some other magic
deep in the heart of God
sure as the rainfall.

But where did they come from,
these dreams?
From our fathers
harsh or gentle
yours or mine
who often took a poor man's existence
and made it rich and expansive,
like éclairs
filled to the point of bursting,
sweet and delicate.
Our fathers who never made promises about life
but simply lived it
or lived it simply,
though with enthusiasm,
until it became manifold and flowing
like a garment regally worn by a noble person,
like the wine aging in the nut-brown barrel,
waiting to bring sparkle to small kitchen tables.

And so here we are,
nuclear children
always on the edge of disaster
or on the threshold of discovery,
searching for the security of yesterday
and the promise of tomorrow.
All the while holding both,
mysteried but available in our hearts,
with the art to sculpt words
and energy to dream dreams
and more than enough reason to say
I love you.

ASHES OF ANOTHER YEAR (Ash Wednesday, 1982)

Sifting through the ashes of another year,
battered beleaguered by a relentless winter,
we tighten the timbre of our lives
and pluck the strings of Lent.
The song is just what we need most of all.
With undulant remembrances
we reach into the sackcloth of our existence,
our accepted time,
and pull out
the warm smell
of hot cross buns and burning palm,
the earnest flavor
of hot crusty bread and thick lentil soup,
sticking to our ribs
clinging to our memories.

Even the choleric snow
becomes an old friend
reluctantly kissing us goodbye at the door
after a warm evening
of glowing wine and crackling fire,
when the empty glasses and smoldering ashes
become
not reasons to mourn
but an opportunity to remember.

The purple thoughts pick their way
through our minds
shimmering
iridescent
and full of promise.
Even if we do not love well
we love the best we can
and are loved in return.

It is irreversible now,
the Springtime light.
Who could deny it welcome?
Who would forestall its arrival?

The years continue to unravel
like an unruly ball of yarn
weaving and whopperjawed before us
but nevertheless madly pursuing their course.
And even in our snowy tombs
there are dreams of delightful gardens,
catalogued and bright,
brave crocuses and defiant daffodils,
pungent dreams
bursting with blossoms and bulbs
and even the subtle hint of sweet basil and parsley.
Who or what can stop us now?
As unyielding as the icy wind of today
are the promises of tomorrow.
Tenacious survivors,
unyielding but penitent,
we plod and lumber toward our prize.

O yes,
we are but dust,
so waft us into the winds of today,
ashes only for now.

PROMISE OF PEACE & GROWTH (New Year's Day, 1983)

The year spins away from us
like a musical top
    —slipping cleverly away
    from the careless hands
    of a little child—
it's music fading and falling
relegated now
to the palaces of memory and reminiscence.

We are left naked
like winter trees
longing for foliage
and fresh greenness.
And while regrets
for things undone
chip in and out of our consciousness
the New Year stands poised
ready to cascade into our lives
and give us another chance.

The unfolding of the days
may be painful or joyful.
But last year's mistakes and memories
become this year's fertile ground
teasing and pulling us
daring us to plant seeds for tomorrow.

Tomorrow
which holds
as if in a nutshell
the promise of
Peace
and Growth.

FOR A FRIEND (1983)

There are those days,
those unspeakable, relentless days
that pillage the peaceable kingdom
of minds teetering on the edge
of conformity.
Those days when I wonder whether
the sand of my oystered life
will ever become
a pearl of any price.

It was such a day
when I opened my home and my heart
  —I live in both and make no distinction
  between the two—
with (cautious) abandon
that blisters and broils beneath
the madcapped and practiced casualness.
And exploding on my
preconceived liberality
  —with all the déjà vu
  of the "wild-eyed windy boy"
  of days gone by—
came a spinning reality
to yo-yo the yesterdays
that had been carefully
rolled and bowled
into a neat ball of twine.
Just when I was sure and comfortable
with little or no thought of change,
possibilities pluralized
into complex diagrammed sentences
and stacked up
like skyscraper ice cream cones
(from my youth)
that ran down the wrists and arms
of carefree children
on warm and sultry summer days.

And pleased to find the old wisdom,
intact and working,
rusty but still precious,
I unfolded the pall of stars
hoping it would make a difference.
I shook out the expanse of sunlight.
Knowing I would always take the chance,
I unleashed the arcing bow of colors
waiting for them to flash back.

All those gifts I had received
undeservedly from lovers and friends
I frenetically unwrapped
knowing the time was short,
grateful for even a moment,
thankful for the rekindling of my own fire.

THE BREAD AND WINE REMAIN (Thanksgiving, 1983)

The Thanksgivings I have known
have always been flavored
with more than the chestnut dressing
that came bursting from the golden turkey.
There were places at table
for widowed aunts and bachelor uncles
and anyone else
who knew there would be a place set
simply because
"no one should be alone on Thanksgiving Day."

And so, it became a way of life...
the extra leaf in the table
the folding chair whisked from the cellar
the "one more glass of wine"
the one more plate, even if it didn't match.
All this pressed something
deep into our hearts and heads.
Before we were Deuteronomied into awareness
to offer the best...we offered all we had.
There was no holding back.
"Is there one more stuffed artichoke?"
"Of course."
Before we were Collossianed into
patience and kindness and mercy
we knew we would wait for the latecomer,
smile at the cousin we didn't even like all that much,
not complain if the platter got emptied
(which it never did).
Returning to say thanks was never an issue
because we never thought of leaving back then.
What did Luke mean: "Where are the other nine?"
They were probably eating mincemeat pie.

Yes, years get tucked into our memory
and nothing remains the same.
The ebb and flow of table fellowship and family gatherings
get white-capped with the burdens of life:
disappointments
hurt
sickness
death.

And still and all
Thanksgiving calls us out of our self-pity and brooding
into the Communion of the Great Banquet.
So if age and time change the dinner companions,
they also crystallize the convictions.
So we search for that extra leaf in the table
that can span the globe...
the plate that can reach across the universe...
the folding chair that can seat the hungry of the world.
    If the cranberry sauce and sweet potatoes should ever run out,
    the Bread and Wine remain.
    Real fellowship, real Thanksgiving, real Presence
    to one another.

ADVENT

Advent
is nothing more or less
than that liminal
slow moving
smooth
night-time
that embraces us
in an inky darkness
so that we have an excuse
to light our meager candles
and wait patiently
for the
Sun of Justice
to explode with
pure light
on our eager
landscape.

THE KEEPERS OF CHRISTMAS (1983)

The year runs out of time
and we run too
(breathless)
looking for a child
to share our burdens
and turn our dreams
into crystals of reality.

This much said,
every year is not the same.
Do you remember Christmases
that came drifting
snowbound and weightless
settling easily and gently
into the present moment
with more than enough
oranges and fruitcake?
And then there were other years
when Christmas
came sneaking quietly
and almost unnoticed
until it erupted on the scene
catching us unaware.
Unwrapping the Christ Child
from a sheet
of last year's newspaper
always brought a shock.
        —He looked the same!
Still other Christmases
came driving relentlessly
down on us
ready or not
screaming
for the last cookie to be pressed
one more gift to be wrapped
the toppled tree to be righted
the final fish to be baked.
We were ready
but not quite
because there would always be
one more thing to do.

Then there will always be those years
when Christmas needs to be dragged
kicking and screaming
from the sealed envelope of a cold December
seemingly trying to avoid time
as we place unrealistic expectations
on such a simple unpretentious day.

This year, some of us needed Christmas
so desperately.
Every bone arched achingly toward the moment
that only a Child could brighten
and only one Man could salvage.
The days of late Autumn seemed endless
with the pain of people
everyday people
real people
on a sometimes desolate
but always hopeful pilgrimage.
We long for so much but need so little.
If our expectations were ever fulfilled
our little shopping bag
would burst at the seams
and all the brightly wrapped packages
would skate away
leaving us with one GIFT.
And still we hope beyond endurance.

Isn't hope the stuff of Christmas
and isn't Christmas its own reward?
When it breaks in on us
(that expansive and immeasurable day)
we laugh at ourselves
(and some cry)
for tithing time as though it were money
and wondering what we did
with our 90 percent.

Who needs a judge
when we've got ourselves,
a people of pinched lips
and prickly principles
plumbing our own depths
and never quite measuring up?

60

We are
too busy with the rules
to enjoy the game.
We are
cautious
furrowed
frozen
by the wind-chill
that rushes ruthlessly
from the chasm of our own emptiness.
Who needs a scorekeeper
to juggle the numbers of our indifference
when we count the cost so carefully
ourselves
making sure to hold on to more than enough
just in case?
What we need is a Child
forced with all the pain of humanity
from the heavy womb of an ordinary woman
—a child whose cry pierces
the wary frugal air
from Bethlehem to Calvary
from then to now
—a child who will not be
Sesame Streeted
into a crib
or haloed into toyland
—a child who is spoken
clearly and concisely
into Manhood by a Father
who will not leave us
to our own demands and devices.

And so we come
sometime shepherds
sometime kings
but always weary travelers
on a road littered with
tramping boots
bloody cloaks
deafening guns.

We come in need of one more Christmas
like that first one
that could not be Caesared and decreed
into being
but only angeled and sung
into life.

Too much for one small Child
one gentle man
now we are the keepers of Christmas.
But like the bread broken
at the family table
it can only nourish us when consumed.
Christmas needs to be thrown and scattered
lavishly about us.
It has been historied into books
but needs to be unwrapped and held up
set free to gust and fly
into the forlorn face
of a fragile fractured world.
We are the keepers of Christmas
—and more.
Poured through the colander of faith
and funneled into fearful waiting hearts
is the spirit of a Man-Child
who makes all the difference
and watches patiently
for the gifts we bring.

Like the rooster that makes the sun rise
We are the keepers of Christmas.
We are the reflecting prism.
We are the flashing truth.
We—beleaguered and blown
like the diamond dusted snow—
We are the keepers of Christmas.

MORE THAN LIFE CAN OFFER (Easter, 1984)

Color
Movement
Life
    Rushing on us
    now unending.
Of the three
one is more difficult
than another
for rain-chilled cold hearts
that prefer to think in
black and white
remaining lifeless
frozen into dormancy.

Spring
inspired
undaunted
nuzzles the chill
from our bones
like a painted pony
from a nursery rhyme
or children's memory.

Remember
childhood memories or a present love
may light the Easter fire
as surely as the pastor's match.
I remember Easter baskets
and warm embraces.
One was cellophaned and bulging
with sweet chocolates and marshmallow chicks.
The other was warm and engulfing
smothering any embarrassment
and lifting a young boy into reality.

Pity the ones with no bright baskets
and no embrace to see them through.
Who will light their fire?
How can they bear death?
How can they know life?

And someone said
"If Jesus were alive today
how unhappy he would be!"
If he were alive…?
Did someone miss something?
But then
some caretakers of despondency
have tried to eulogize him into calling hours.

How little they know
just how much death
we can sustain
with life assured in the final foray.
Who says there are no guarantees?
With the trees greening into May
and the grass swelling from the sodden tomb
we have a promise for tomorrow
more pleasing than
an invitation to Easter dinner.

Does the Word proclaimed
give meaning to life
or does life give life
to the Word instead?
        —A gift exchange no doubt.
We strain to catch the light
erupting from the candle-pillar
that slices the devil's food darkness.
We plunge a ladling heart
like a cupped hand
into the waters of our future
that wash away the doom
of living with the past.

Answers lie
in that water tomb
that watery womb
from which we emerge
sparkling and drenched.
The dike of unspeakable love
breaks
and we are flooded,
awash in grace.

Answers lie
in the oozing oil
rubbed into our souls
chrismed into our hearts.

Finally
repeatedly
crusty bread
rises above encrusted hearts
and both bread and hearts
are Eastered with new life.
This Eucharist
is not defined
in the stiffly bound books
on the neat and numbered shelves
in some musty theological library.
Rather
Eucharist finds meaning
in the sun-drenched kitchens
        —with littered counter-tops
        and flour sprinkled tables—
where children learn the lessons of life
and how to care for one another.

Awesome initiation
into more than life can offer.
And we do it again and again and again.
Alleluia!

WHAT DID I GIVE? (Dominican Sisters' Jubilee, 1984)

If getting there is half the fun
my life has been a barrel of laughs.
If getting there is half the battle
my life has been a third world war.
Usually I arrive
a little late
itching to get started,
wondering
on bad days
what I will give.
Life, life.
One day somersaulting
soaring
racing
sun glittered and green.
Another day limping
dragging
droning
overcast and grey.
Leaving home,
calling home,
where is home?

"Religious Life?"
they asked,
(curiously or critically)
"Why would you do that?"
Don't ask me.
I was just an innocent bystander
but here I am.
God's call, remember?
Community prayer
community life
community ministry.
Some time alone
        —that would be nice.
But no loneliness please.
Something snaps in my eyes
where tears are bottled away
for a rainy day.
And then I laughed so hard
my stomach hurt.

And there was a flash
a memory
déjà vu
of stifling that chapel giggle.
Has it been that long?
A good year here.
A bad year there.
Another year with that one!
Is she talking to me?
And before the years of Excedrin too!
And yet,
maybe the bad years
were the good years.

Haven't I changed?
And I never even noticed.
Did I get better
or just older?
And what did I give?
Time?
I seem to have so little.
Talent?
That's limited.
I guess I only gave myself
sometimes willingly
sometimes grudgingly.
Some days I poured myself out
free and flowing,
sweet water from the rock.
Other days I only oozed myself out
like cold molasses, clinging to itself.
But who's finished anyway?
And what did I give
is a question for the end of the journey.
For now I think I will just keep moving.
Silver and Gold Jubilee?
No, rather
flesh and blood celebration.
With a large dose of the spirit
to keep it alive.
What did I give?
Ask me tomorrow
after today has been celebrated.
Ask me tomorrow.

THIS SACRAMENT IS A CIRCLEMENT (Wedding, 1984)

You can never go home again
they say.
And it is true, no doubt.
That place where hearts are borne
on wings of laughter
and subtle love
takes on an illusiveness
so complete as to escape
return, remorse or revenge.
But some little boys
winsome and bedeviled
slow or sleek
grow into bright-eyed young men
with a vision no one can
darken, diminish or take away.
And they create new spaces and places
hand to hand
with a woman
sprung vibrant and alive
from the soul of a little girl
lost or loved
cradled or independent
but arriving nonetheless
at a place in time
where the eye of love
and the heart of flesh and blood
bring warmth to winter
and coolness to summer.

And now
while the Autumn olive is
red and ripe and ready
for plucking by the wild birds
with music in their wings
a new home is built
not with brick and board
but rather readiness
and will
and commitment
and even tears.

As the landscape of yesterday
flies into the shining sky
horizoned beyond our reach
a new environment is sprung up
blossoming into Spring
greening into Summer
coloring into Fall
crisping into Winter.
And this new place
is planted and peopled
with friendly faces and strong trees
transplanted
transformed
and having new life.
For a Sacrament is a circlement
going out
coming back
widening its diameter
encompassing more than any one person can embrace
providing enough love for everyone
who dares to step into the ring
set aflame by two people
fanned by the Spirit
fed by humanity.
This sacrament is a circlement
that leaves space
for new ideas
new faces
and wonderful surprises.
This sacrament is what we need
most of all
for it keeps nothing to itself
but arches out beyond expected reaches
across waters of fear
seas of disaster
and deserts of loneliness.
And so another link is clasped
on the chain of promise
dangling and dropping
within our grasp
held firmly at its origin and source
by the Hand of Love.

HIS PRESENCE REMAINS (Christmas, 1984)

For stargazers and seekers
there is a light
that streaks
with relentless hope
even across dark skies of sadness
and despair
penetrating all the world with
brightness.
Even when the eye of winter
glances off September
and comes piercing
premature
into November,
it prevails.
Oh yes
the brightness prevails.

Still
when they say
"There's no place like home
for the holidays"
it remains true
that for some
even at Christmas
the brightness is blocked
and home is a wounded
hurting heart
hungering more for healing
than fruitcake or plum pudding.
Home is a sealed heart
waiting to be opened
    —by some grace—
and flowered
    —as if in a vase.
Who has not sat at table
on Christmas
when an absence
or an empty chair
cried out louder than angels
for peace and goodwill?

And who has not shuddered and shook
like a broken-winged bird
at the thought of a heart
        —another's or your own—
hardened like frozen earth
crunching and flaking
under those squeaking rubber boots?
A heart that cannot
forgive or be forgiven.
A heart looking for a mangered child
but embracing only
the straw and illusion
of unrealistic expectations
and vague dreams.

When I was little
with a poet's heart
but no words in my mouth
I thought Christmas was people
who countered the winter winds
with gales of laughter
that came rolling across
the sea of enthusiasm
spread with the tablecloth
on the Christmas groaning board
that held us close
and fed our spirits as well as our bodies.

One year I cried
because I was afraid
Christmas wouldn't find me.
The snow was billowing and blowing
and my stocking
didn't have a name on it
and looked so much like any other.
The neighbor kids
each had a Woolworth's special stocking
all fuzzy and red and white
with their names
glittering from the cuff
with sequins and sparkles.
I was sure mine would be lost
in the cotton shadows of ordinariness.

Even though I was too old
to believe in Santa Claus
I was young enough to hope for the best.
Then someone told me
the stocking didn't matter
and a severe nun
in a moment of tenderness
said there was a star in the sky
with my name on it.
And so all the way to midnight Mass
with the piquant odor
of smelt and codfish
suspended in my nostrils
I pressed my face
against the frosted back seat window
of the old green Kaiser
and looked for that special star
or maybe the one that
blinded the wise men
to the dirt and dinginess of old Bethlehem.
I was sure I found it once
but thought I was mistaken
when it came to rest
over the sooty steel mill
hunkered down in the valley
by the muddy river
that never froze
no matter how cold.
Poor lost star
looking for Bethlehem
but settling for a blast furnace.
Still the light from the blast furnace
or the star
        —I can't remember which—
flickered and darted
across the steely slate-grey sky
and framed the old stone church
on the hill
making it look more beautiful
than the white New England churches
in the Currier and Ives Christmas cards
better even than the little church
on the calendar from the bank.

Sister said,
as she tightened too much
the big red bow around my neck
that men fire the furnaces
and God glitters the stars
but each light has its own purpose
and brightens the world
so Jesus knows
where heaven and earth
work together to light His way.

We marched in straight linen lines
red cassocks and white surplices
floating like sailboats
over the smooth swirling snow.
We marched with heads erect
pretending we were kings
but knowing who we really were.
The organ rolled like thunder
out of the Christmased heavens.
The voices surged and swelled.
The incense puffed and flew away
as if on an urgent mission.
Adeste Fidelis...
and we did.
Jubilate Deo...
and we did.
Introibo ad altare Dei...
and we did.

Then robed and rowed
in the smooth endless pews
we settled down and listened
one more time to the old tale
about Caesar Augustus and Joseph and Mary
wondering if the ending would be different this year.
But the words of the familiar story
reassured us once again
as they escaped
unbounded
from the big red book
and flew into our bones
like arrows and angels.

Christmas struck its roots
deeper into the soil of our souls
and grew another year.

Magic and miracles were the same
for a young boy.
Back home again
the little Christ appeared
as always
in his special place under the tree
and watched us open presents
in the wrapping strewn living room.

Then the hour and the excitement
filled my head with
convoluted cobwebs
that wound their way through my mind
as I watched the little plaster statue
asleep in the hay.
And one more Christmas Eve
skated away
across the pond of fond memories
to be mosaiced in our minds.
Then we slept
heartened and cheered
with the security of knowing
that when
the presents
      are opened,
His presence
      remains.

For stargazers and seekers
there really is a light
that streaks with relentless hope
even across dark skies...
penetrating all the world with
Brightness.

GOD OF EXTRAVAGANT LOVE (Easter, 1985)

Shrugging suspiciously
out of winter layers
we move with pent-up excitement
through the throes of Lent.
Believing in sunshine
at this trying time
of the yearning year
requires more faith
than believing in wild resurrection.
Or so it seems.
The wind and the weather-vane
vacillate
from one extreme to the other.
We do too.
We do too.
Now hot.
Now cold.
Pointing here.
Pointing there.

Even crocuses are careful.
How can they be sure
as they purple out of the crusty earth?
They take their stand, such as it is,
low and tenacious
braving the unknown
heralding the hopeful.
We are more hesitant than crocuses
helping
ourselves to a sliver of the kingdom
hoarding
our story
hiding
our vulnerability
under a Lenten blanket
of meager sacrifices and stationed crosses
that we choose carefully
and place at strategic spots
on our Easter route.
Forgetting God's initiative
we congratulate ourselves
on a Lent well-kept.

But like the sap
running in the sugar maple
nothing can hold back
the sweet flowing waters of life
not even our unimaginative self-esteem.
The God of abundant surprises
the God of extravagant love
the God of generous life
has more than enough imagination
for all of us put together.

I remember when Holy Week was spent
in the Church
or in the kitchen.
Incense and anise vied
for a place of honor
in my olfactory memory.
As we kneaded the enormous vat
of rising dough
we wondered if 16 loaves would be enough
to satisfy the tabled Easter appetites
of travelers from Lent
who tired of lentil soup
or pasta and beans.

So in the kitchen
as much as in the sanctuary
I learned of the magnitude of God's care for us.
He always has enough
of what we need the most
to satisfy our appetite
and fill the measuring cup of love.
But that love is so incredible!
In this day of trivial pursuits
post-teen marriages
and self-centered arrangements
we are especially thrilled
when we encounter two people
whose love is not stifling, exclusive and turned in
but creative, all embracing and outgoing.
I know a few such lovers.

Their names are indelibly penned
on the soft brown parchment
of my scrolled heart.
But usually we are skeptical of love
because of the limits our humanity sets.

It is no wonder
we are grateful then
for a love so enduring
that it survives, no, defeats death
and creates a new world
for the Mary Magdalenes
who know their capacity for loving
in spite of empty tombs
and mislaid bodies.

Like rabbits out of hats
gardeners invariably appear
touching our tears
recognizing our pain
calling our name
giving us our identity again.
In flowing water and flickering flame
we discover who we are.
We invite others
to join us at font and fire.
Only together do we have a future
to lean into.
They cup their hearts
to receive the water
and hold their fire aloft.
We are all once again
washed and ignited.

Can we become like John of the Gospel?
Love made the beloved disciple
jump at once to the right conclusion:
Jesus is alive.
So our lives are full of sights and sounds
lovers and friends
people and events
that make us cry out:
It is the Lord.
It is the Lord.

DARKNESS DISPELLED (Christmas, 1985)

If Virgil
or Homer
or even Emily Dickinson
had a Muse
they have kept her for themselves
this year.
We must have our own you know.
I have waited
anxiously
frantically
painfully
this Christmas
but she never appeared.
On a sensible sabbatical no doubt.
Even inspiration needs a holiday.

We all know the feeling
when "Merry Christmas"
or even "Good Morning"
is replaced
by long sympathetic lines
of silent friends
people past and present
who want to hold your heart
warm it
and take the loneliness away.
But alas
we all know
it cannot be
and death
like life
must take hold of us
and become a friend.
Even a flood of tears
cannot wash away the sorrow
or fill the empty space.
We are blessed
if the tears
do not cast upon the shore
of our indifference
the flotsam and jetsam
of regrets or love unspoken.

How odd
that when
bereft of inspiration
the Scriptures become our last resort
instead of the first.
And there
blaring from the page
louder than any trumpet
clearer than any bell
more resonant than any pipe
Isaiah proclaims the darkness dispelled
and gives perspective to our pessimism.
Humanity
left to its own undoing
is doomed to despair.

A Currier and Ives Christmas
like this one
with the sky flaking into lace
and floating like down
dolloping like cream
is a fluke of nature
a chance happening
fickle and beyond control
beyond planning.
But darkness dispelled
by a God-friend
taking on flesh
joining our joy
sharing our sorrow—
NOW THAT IS A THING OF PLANNING!
Revelation unfolds
not by chance
but by design.
No happenstance
no innocent bystanders
no unrelated spirits.
Every life
every death
is crucial and required.

You notice
the angels returned to heaven.
They went home.

But we shepherds were left
and a few wise men too.
Without benefit of wings
we must trudge
through life and death itself
to the place of birth.
We must search
for the child
so that we too
may see and understand.

Now
as then
all who hear are astonished
if the WORDS pierce
the space between
page and heart
and make an impression in warm flesh.
If a little blood is drawn
so be it.

Mary's treasuring heart
is the model.
It is unlikely
she smiled demurely
at the darkness and poverty
of her delivery room.
Do you believe
she cast a desultory or passive
eye
upon her son's ministry
and pain?
Could she calmly
placidly
hold a dying child
against a soundless bosom
and sweetly accept
birth and death
without a murmur?
No doubt
she was a
Fellini Madonna.

A human mother
who raged and screamed
with all the pent-up passion
of the Jewish People
who streamed for centuries
toward salvation and peace
only to be surprised
to receive more
than they ever dared desire.

With Eliot* we wonder
is it birth or death we celebrate?
Or are they not the same?

When at birth
the cord is cut
and we are set to soar
free and unrestrained
we immediately begin
tying our own knots
so as not to be alone.
And so there is
a strain
a string
a bond
that sustains us.
And the Christmas child
is a gauntlet
thrown down before the darkness
that cannot win the joust.

We celebrate the victory
as best we can
decorating our lives
using even tinsel
to get us through the night.
Extending our family.
Lengthening our table.
Filling our stomachs.
Hoping our spirits will be satisfied.
With joyful strains
of colorful carols
we sing away the blackness
and welcome the light.

We bake the cookies
hoping to sweeten our lives.
We sign the cards
yearning for someone to know our name.
We light the candles
hoping to see a flame in another's eye.
We open packages
wanting most of all
to unwrap our hearts.

With unflinching strength
and unwavering vigor
Christmas has sustained
the weight of the centuries.
Humanity unbound
embraces a child
and discovers instead
in its arms
Promise for tomorrow
and Peace for today.

(* T.S. Eliot's poem "Journey of the Magi")

A HOME FOR EVERYONE (Christmas, 1986)

I wonder if Joseph ever felt
that there were those days
when his life
was a rambling rushing sentence
with no punctuation
but only verbs and adjectives
exploding from the pen of the mind
finding no rest
on the clean white paper of life.

But then
he was a simple man
unarmed with the luxury of worry.
Or were those dreams
not really dreams
but rather his own anxious reverie
born of the unwavering wrestling
with his own thoughts
as he searched for a bed
because his hand felt the life move
in her swollen stomach?
Could there be a home for them?

And she,
wrenched from her father's house
set on the road
hapless pilgrim
with a confusion too deep
to give way to guilt
wondering where she would weep
over a child born into a hostile world.
She desperately needed a home,
a home to have
a home to provide.
The two of them
unlikely pilgrims
trailing the night
unsettling the flocks
scrambling the stars
leaving a wake of hope
as they sliced their way
through the darkness.

The stars stopped spinning.
The flocks stopped bleating.
A flurry of angels burst
on the scene
when finally
the homeless couple
gouged out a hole in the darkness
and filled the cavity with light
as the babe screamed his way
into brightness.
And in that lustrous brilliance
they discovered
that all the while
beneath her racing heart
Mary had carried a home for everyone.

NEWS OF HOPE (Easter, 1987)

Paul Simon says:
"Losing love is like a window in your heart.
Everybody sees you're blown apart.
Everybody feels the wind blow."*

It has been
it seems
a hurricane season
with penetrating winds
for a long long time.
Losing love
is not the same as
losing lovers.
Losing love
is that dying that compresses all the air
from your billowing sails
and leaves you hanging high and helpless
over foaming seas.
Losing love
is that dying that prevails
when life unfolds in wrinkles and creases
when your stomach is a swinging wrecking ball
when your brain is blunt and uncolored
when your heart stands suspended
and ready to drop.
Losing love is the crashing crushing conviction
that someone expects more than you have
that you expect the impossible
and that everyone is doomed to disappointment.
Losing love is knowing
that the door to your mother's kitchen
is locked forever
and life is a desperate search
for a golden loaf of Easter Bread
more elusive than the Holy Grail.

Only in that knowing
can the Paschal Mystery
—a new life—
erupt inside your heart
in the very window left open
by the loss of love.

85

Certainly Judas was somebody's lover
and it could have been enough.
So even in the face of losing love
    new fire
    new water
    new words
    new life
explode like honeyed sun
filling the window panes
with bright yellow rays.
And anyone can learn to fly again.

Has it only been a year
since I pondered this?
Life is only short when looking backward.
But in process
it is an eternal now.

Can we respond
with full hearts
—in spite of lost love—
to the dawning before us?
Can the God who led Israel
through the desert
lead us to the shore of tomorrow?
Can the Lord who brought
water from the rock
fountain each of us to life again?

I am ready for the earthquake
that will blow the boulder away
and send angels like lightening
to sit and talk a while.
I am ready for the word of Peace
that will ignite an unyielding flame in me.
Losing love eliminates fantasy
so that reality can root
and mystery us into Paschal Life.

And so the Rhythm of our Communal Heart
is the steady beat
of an ALLELUIA
that leaves us
—not with an empty tomb—
but with an abiding presence
that urges us on
with news every heart
is thundering to proclaim.
News of promise.
News of hope.
"Peace."
"Don't be afraid."
"They will see me."

*(*from "Graceland" by Paul Simon)*

A PLACE REVISITED (Ursuline High School, 1987)

Hallowed halls have ways of narrowing
over the years.
It is like going home again
and the dining room table seems so small.
And why was the journey
from 309 to 124
a trauma in those days
of tardy slips and hall monitors?
It seems like such a short distance today
with no familiar faces to slow me down.
(I would welcome one.)
Maybe the miles we log
pale our perspective
as our limited life
expands from neat little packages
to monumental structures
and complicated patterns
that we can no longer
unwrap at will.

There was a sense of accomplishment
when I could hypotenuse myself
from Trig to Latin in 4 minutes
and shift from parallelograms
to declensions
without a hitch.
And if I can't remember
which meeting I must attend tonight
I can still recite
the Prologue of the Canterbury Tales
in Middle English.

Today the sea of students
swallowed en masse
by the hungry cafeteria
is no less animated than we were.
There are things that don't change.
But people do. People do.

And the colors in our eyes
—always so black and white back then—
now come in a myriad of hues
because the years add
pigment and shading
unknown to us in 1960
when life was an
untouched canvas.

ASK FOR A STAR (Christmas, 1987)

Like Caesar Augustus and George Gallup
we do little good with the information gathered
but continue to log our statistics
review our research
and keep one another in tow.
Insatiable computers
with all buttons and no brains,
could it be heart
we lack and look for?
Tired Tin Man lost in Oz,
counting heads is useless
when hearts are left
untended or unchanged.

Today is not a day for
numbers or numbness.
We are inspirited into oneness
and Decembered into feeling.
There is nothing beyond and beside
ourselves
now that God has taken up
residence within.
Still we wait and look
while the search does not promise
to take us far away
but rather offers a journey
deeper and deeper
into a reality so simple and so huge.

The silent tongue-tied days
of Advent waiting
give way now, ready or not
to the exquisite prose
and speechless poetry of Christmas.
The frenetic pace of preparation is,
in fact,
a labored, lumbering walk
compared to the
spritely dancing of the Day of the Lord.

When we are finally sugar-plummed
out of childhood and make-believe
we find that
Stars and Light
never take away the blackness
but simply show a way
through the gloom
and around the chunks of darkness.

The tired, the sick, the crippled and the aged
do not experience
a televangelist healing
compliments of your
favorite TV network
but rather receive
a modest portion of hope
for the future
and the simple blessing
of memories of Christmas past.

So early early
we crash into the unexpected truth
that the baby we would hold
is a dying man
who simply walks with us
more silently than a snowflake falls.
But it is reason to rejoice
because the company alone
is worth the trip.

O yes,
sing a song,
dance if you like.
Ask for a star.
Our future is not determined
by what we receive tomorrow.
No,
our future is secured
by what we believe today.

THE PULL TOWARD PENTECOST (1988)

Easter
pulls the plug
and empties out
all self-absorption,
making space
for positive energy
that sends us
bursting forth,
rising,
strengthening,
flying,
soaring high above
our limited selves.
Like a new bride,
believers are overcome with
new life
security
promise
hope.
We look to one another,
drawn from the depth of dream
waking to
transformation,
feeling an almost
laser-like loveliness
penetrating our old blood.
We look to one another
with amazement and wonder and gratitude
for this marvelous God.
We look to one another...

ST JOSEPH, MANTUA FAREWELL (July 24, 1988)

Most of us move
quietly, unnoticed,
into the faceless crowd
clutching our little
loaf of bread,
hoping for the best or,
if not the best,
at least to be left alone.

Didn't the lad with the barley loaves
have enough on his mind?
Probably away from home
on his way
to who knows where,
looking for work, maybe,
or a new adventure.

But now this gaggle
of itinerant preachers
is asking him to share his bread.
Didn't they know it was
painful enough already, scary,
being
on your own
on the road
on the way?

In the taking of his bread
—a wrenching loss for a frightened boy—
he discovered
the giving of a community of faith.
In the middle of nowhere
he found a home,
a place to be,
people to embrace.

And so once again
having pushed my little car
faithfully,
yesterdaying it
through tears and smiles,
I shift gears
and hope that
tomorrow's seasons will be cycled
with enough happiness
to see me through.

At the place we stand
the road always looks
wide and broad,
but up ahead,
on the horizon,
it narrows to a nothingness,
a point
through which we think
we'll never pass.
But we do, we do.

Leaving behind
the faces and the places
where you have shared life and death,
birth and burials,
is a kind of death itself.
But if memories of
mothers and fathers
gone before us in happiness,
with wry humor,
can sustain us,
so the thoughts of places
left behind can bring a smile.

Early on
without really knowing it
I learned to seize life
with a fury,
Calabrese style
and without regret.

O yes,
there is a sadness
in leaving rolling fields
—even in a drought.
Who would exchange
furrowed rows and flowing rivers
for a malled existence
tended by towering steel fossils
from childhood memory?

But there is a road
ribboned and winding,
and so I rummage furiously
through my knapsack
looking for a special loaf
to feed a new hunger.
If a lad can feed five thousand
I must have something to offer.
If only they will take it
and multiply it
into something of substance,
hardy and crusty.

Besides my knapsack,
I carry an expanse of fabric,
memory cloth,
cradling the names of those who have
transformed the faceless crowd
into a living canvas
that can be hung securely
on the walls of my heart.

We may not have learned
all the lessons well,
but we know,
with a deep-down determination,
dancing the loneliness away,
that in gathering for bread
there is no room for goodbyes
or separation.
For in the giving and taking
of this Bread,
no matter where we stand,
there is one Lord, one Faith.

ITALY FROM THE TRACKS (1988)

Glinting down the tracks
from Naples to Sicily,
watching the towns fly by the window
of the rumbling rambling train,
my face pressed to the glass,
my eye devouring every inch
of the landscape,
I saw the whispering moon
step slowly up the sky-scape.
It came to rest over the waters off the shore of Calabria.
As that shimmering golden sphere
slow-motioned its voyage
something pulled me into love.
Something unseen and even unknown,
drew me into a relationship
like I had never experienced before.

SAVUTO: ON GOING HOME (1988)

Lurching up that ancient mountain road
—to the obscure village of Savuto—
clinging tenaciously to the vertical landscape,
I thought of my father,
wondering how often his feet
had picked and plodded their way
along this route.
Then, looking out the tiny window
of the chugging Fiat
I saw the Calabrian Sun
searing the atmosphere,
lighting up the rock formations,
glistening the leaves of the olive and scrub trees.
And I knew in an instant
where the light had gone
from my father's eyes
in the end.

It had streaked its way back here,
back home,
to flicker and dart
in the old familiar places,
like the light
that flies from the eyes
of so many of our old people.
Not really disappearing
but simply lighting up some other place.
And there is comfort in that,
in knowing that the present
is somehow illumined
by the old lights,
by the past.
The new is truly enlightened by the old.

With these webs weaving
through my mind,
I arrived at last
at the poor little piazza,
expecting what?
A familiar face?
My own eyes staring back at me
from the face of another?

Who knows?
Our inquiries scared up
a little rabbit of a woman
whose face was like home to me.
She was like a family portrait,
a group picture,
carrying in one body
the image of an entire clan.
On that mountain,
in those poor buildings,
in her face,
I discovered a home I never knew I had.

Looking at me incredulously
she pulled me down the old street,
pulled me down the years,
pulled me into my own history.
She drew me into a doorway,
into a home,
familiar but never seen before.

In that room
were the craggy faces
of home.
Out that kitchen window
were the craggy mountains
        (faces themselves)
of home,
burned bright by the warming sun
of home.
Looking around
I could see in a glance
all that they had.
And it was enough.

INTO ETERNITY

I remember you
I do
I do.
And you remember me too
don't you
don't you?

You will hold me
in your heart
remember me
put me together again
if I ever fall apart.

I will remember you
into eternity
and so you will
always be
always be
always be.

We are here to
remember.
And memory is
you see
the ability
to create from the past
a sense of meaning in the present
and also
the joyful
        exciting
        vibrant
anticipation of possibility
in days to come
in our future
in the forever
that opens before us.

REMEMBERING JOE: "My Little Brother"

Joseph Angelo Fata was many things to many people—but to me, he was my little brother. He was the baby of our family, younger brother to Anthony and me. We had NINETEEN first cousins and he was— you got it—the youngest of those too. You probably know where I'm going with this. He was spoiled—there, I said it!

While he never lorded it over us, Joey was the prince. Of course maybe Mom and Dad were just protecting him from us! There was that time I dropped him on his head—it took Mom a while to get over that one! And then the time we accidently weaned him from bottle feedings...When Joey was 8 months old, our parents left Anthony (age 12) and me (age 6) to babysit. We were to give Joey a bottle, burp him, and put him down to sleep. He only slept about 30 minutes before he woke up crying. So, we tried all of Mom's tricks. We changed his diaper, rocked him, sang to him, and then laid him back down to sleep—not happening—so Anthony suggested another bottle, which Joey eagerly drank. We laid him in his crib (again), he slept (sorta) about 20 minutes and resumed crying. We tried this same routine two more times. My parents came home after the fourth bottle. Mom was talking softly and gently patting his back. Soon we all heard a loud noise, and a Niagara Falls of milk came out, then a few more burps, and he fell asleep in Mom's arms. We had forgotten about burping him, and he never took another bottle after that night!

Joey was "spoiled" with love, which gave him a quiet (and at times not-so-quiet) confidence. Growing up, we all had our chores, and Joe proudly did his share. It was our job to wash and dry the supper dishes. He was always bugging me to let him wash, and when I asked him why he wanted to switch, he answered calmly and surely, "because I can get them cleaner than you, and I won't make such a mess." He was only eight—shades of things to come! Yes, Joey could be infuriating (we all know this), but he was smart, generous, passionate...I loved to make him laugh, enjoy a glass of wine with him, bring him my sauce or jam or pizzelles...Mostly, I was proud and blessed to have him as my little brother.

—Mickey Fata

CHAPTER FOUR
ST. LUKE, BOARDMAN (1989-1999)

JOSEPH'S TREASURE CHEST (1989)

Everybody needs a box,
a special chest for saving things,
a place for treasures, toys and books,
old photographs and bits of string.

It has to be a private place,
where just anyone cannot go,
a place that everyone respects,
even though they'd love to know,

just what it is he saves and keeps,
and what it is he puts in there,
those birthday cards, notes and letters,
they'd love to read but wouldn't dare.

So this is Joseph's special place,
where he can keep what he thinks best.
And only he can look inside,
'cause this is Joseph's Treasure Chest.

THE HEART IS A HARBOR (Valentine's Day, 1990)

The Heart
is not a cure
for hiding
to lament separation
or lost Love.
O no!
The Heart
is a harbor
where friends and strangers
    can drop anchor
    can leave tossing waves
    can find peace.
The Heart
is a harbor
where even the ship of a fool
moors calmly
trading the hurricane
of disquietude
for the warm breeze
of Love.

BLESSINGS (1991)

The bones
of our mothers
and fathers
indeed all
who have loved us
are like
white doves
that perch
in the black
El Greco trees
of our
consciousness
ready to fly
into our
present moment
when we need
to remember
who we are
when we need
to know
where we came from
when we need
to be sure
that the hearts
we hold dear
are
the most precious
blessings.

FOR JOE FIALA (January 4, 1992)

(Joe knew the rules, and so he will not be expecting a eulogy.
Eulogies are not part of our faith tradition.
But he also knew that, in times of great emotions,
reflections and words serve me well.
So he might be expecting this.)

If wise men and kings
can skate off across
the winter-layered landscape
in search of a brighter star,
then why can't a prince of a man
like Joe?

T.S. Eliot said
the Magi didn't know
whether they were led
all that way
for Birth or Death.
We know it is the same.
And the journey continues.

We might be tempted
to compare Joe to a light in our lives,
a brief flash
or a slow comet!
But he was neither.
He was just one of us,
one like us,
and that makes it all the worse,
and all the better.

Blessed is that man
who takes seriously
the command to share himself,
to unleash himself
on an aching world.
Christ did that you know.
Isn't it him of whom we speak?

He was not a raging bull
of a man
and so he moved quietly among us,
smiling a shy smile,
all the while
slicing off
bits and pieces
even chunks
of himself,
his spirit.
No eulogy, remember.
It is Christ of whom we speak.

And he was a quiet man of passion
who loved us more than we knew.
He fed us so well.
He celebrated with us so easily.
He even gave us life.
It is Jesus, remember.

We learned
how to move beyond ourselves
and found that we had
gifts to offer.
Gifts we had received.
Gifts that far outstripped
the garish gold
the feeble frankincense
the meager myrrh.

And it was a gift exchange
a trading of love.
Don't forget of whom we speak.

Yes,
we found gifts.
Gifts!
I know well what I have received.
God has never spoken
directly to me
nor handed me a gift in person.
No.

God has always used what and who
is at hand
to speak a word
to offer a gift
to transform
to love me out of myself.
First I got from my father
Spirit and life.
I wonder if he knew.
From my mother
I took blood and breath.
She didn't mind.
Then the showers and sun of April
gave me a love for life
     —new life, change
     —new flowers, beauty.
It is a rich month
and could afford the gift.

But as I grow
they keep coming to me,
oddly packaged
or delicately wrapped,
the gifts keep coming.
Hearts and hands,
love and friendship,
unearned and undeserved,
like Grace itself.
They keep coming to me.
To you too, don't you think?

And so
this December man
sturdy and ever-green
in his love for us,
uncompromising too
  —though you would never know—
this December man
wonderfully wintered
in a blanket of simplicity,
grew like a tree among us
and took his place,
planted in our very soil.
Do you know who I mean?

Then he leaves us
—once again—
with the perennial questions:
Who will bake the Bread?
Who will make the Wine?
But we know.

This December man
seems to have vanished
from our sorrow-filled landscape
at the beginning of our aching year.

So, yes,
we follow those kings
and a prince of a man.
We reach for a star
and hang on for dear life,
mourning our losses,
shedding our tears,
knowing deep down
it is Birth we pursue
not death.
Knowing deep down
it is Birth we shall have,
by the Light of a Star.

JOHN THE BAPTIST (1992)

Locusts and wild honey
are never enough to fill
the hunger of centuries
and so
after waiting beyond human endurance
filled with longing
by desert emptiness
John the Baptizer
came raging from the sylvan barrenness
shaking his mane
roaring his message
looking
      —like the lion from Isaiah's prophecy—
for a child to love
and maybe even carry on his back
into the hostile civilization
that had never known
desert growth
and wilderness peace.

Straightening paths
filling valleys
and leveling mountains
is the work of bulldozers
rather than peacemaking men
like Jesus.
And so
John scooped up the
dirt of decades
and scattered it to the
wild wind
so that some few at least
could see the Light of God
setting aside the darkness
while the Herald himself
slipped off into oblivion
maybe returning
to dare the desert into greenness.

THE HEART OF MEMORY (Valentine's Day, 1992)

Something beautiful
can carry you
not because of its beauty
—no—
because of your connectedness.
It draws you out.
It offers life beyond
the breath you breathe.
It is life becoming love.

Then it carves and fashions
a story in your heart.
And the stories we tell
have a way
of taking care of us.
We only think we take care of
and treasure our stories
but oh no
it isn't so.
Our stories breathe on their own.
They take care of us
keep us.

Carefully
we plant the story
in our memory
in each other's memory
for we know
deep down we do
that we need stories
more than food.

So it is
that what is beautiful
now captured in the story
can carry you to the end.

A DAY IN MAINE (1992)

Before I knew
that sounds
could press pictures
into words
I learned to take
a slice of the sun
into my nights.
There is never
sadness in a sunset,
no mourning
for a day gone-by
as the final moments
flash-flood into colors
squeezed from the tube
by the sea and the mountain.

Now listen to the moon
strum softly
the white strings of light
across the flannel sky.
Notes on my staff of life
symphonied
with metronome needles
as my mother knits away the chill
stretching long-muted metaphors
into enormous afghans
that kept us warm
between forays into the attic
to retrieve the bittersweet maple creams
(always a five-pound box)
in the pastel-swirled wrapping
surreptitiously placed
for "safe-keeping"
on grocery day.

And when it rained
(those chill-to-the-bone rains)
I pretended I was a schooner
from a history book page,
arrowing, slashing the salty waters,
yellow slicker shining,
my armor.

Jackson Street was Nova Scotia
and for all sailors
home was the harbor
piered, boardwalked, and barnacled
with warm sounds
secure scenes
flavorful life
and familiar books
where frightened boys and girls
hang their lives out to dry,
retrieve the seascape of the day,
and relive their short history.

AN ORDINARY LIFE (May 25, 1993)   Mark 5:18-20

They weren't nearly as amazed as I am.
Just as the man in the Gospel
discovered that following Christ
meant trudging back
to the same old places
he had been before,
but with a new vision,
so I have come to know
that the mysterious vocation
the sisters told me about
is really a call
to live an ordinary life
with ordinary people
but with an extra-ordinary vision.

And so we can look
birthing
living and
dying straight in the eye
and keep on moving.
When life is an exhilarating balance
on a high wire
stretched over canyons
of enthusiasm and joy
        —it is ordinary.
When life is a bottomless plummet
into oceans of sadness
littered with
the flotsam and jetsam of death
        —it is ordinary.
When life is an endless wait
in the void of aloneness
blackened by hopelessness
        —it is ordinary.
It is ordinary because no one is spared.
It is ordinary because each one is blessed.

But vision makes the difference.
For Sirach ordinariness is wondrous.
For Zephaniah ordinariness is the Lord
in our midst.

How is it for you?
How is it for you?
I am just an ordinary man
standing among ordinary people
screaming for just a little
amazement.
Some of us can do that, you know!
25 years
>   laughing, crying
>   singing, dying
>   running, crawling
>   pushing, stalling
>   giving, taking
>   mending, breaking
>   coming, going
>   doubting, knowing
>   changing, saving
>   getting, craving
>   losing, finding
>   holding, binding
>   loving, hating
>   rushing, waiting.
25 ordinary years
screaming for just a little
amazement.

The idealized, romantic
following of Christ
has been, after all,
a journey back to my own people
just to tell them
what the Lord has done for me.
And so we are still on the road.
Still quite ordinary
and just a little amazed.

(This reflection was written as a homily for liturgy to celebrate Joe's 25th Year of Ordination, and it was read at his funeral almost 25 years later.)

COME INTO LIFE (Easter, 1994)

This was one of those years
one of those
"few and far between" years.
One of those
"I can't believe it's snowing again" years.
One of those
"Remember the Winter of 93?" years.
One of those years
when the season throws a net
of woven cutting cold ice
over our lukewarm lives
and chills the hell out of us
to make room for a bit of heaven.

"Who feels like baking Easter bread
when it is snowing?" she said.
And, in a flash, a crocus
screamed to the surface.
And she began the ritual again.
Like giving birth.

Dying and rising
like icicles and daffodils
are unpredictable
and sometimes out of sync.

Old deaths and new deaths
mix together in our collective bowl
to make a loaf that is
heavy with tears
yet tasty and nourishing
like life itself.

Who can really understand it?
The women didn't.
They came prepared for
stone and death
cold and callous
and funeral rites to soothe their loss.

What they found,
bewildering and challenging,
was an Opening,
a passage into another world
and more life than
they could bear.

Who can really understand it?
The men couldn't.
Maybe that's why the women
kept it to themselves at first.
They knew
how unbelief
and fear
and skepticism
get a stranglehold
on fickle-minded folks
who would rather face death
and call it courage.
Try life!
That's heroism.

It is true
as the young angel-man said:
"You shouldn't be amazed."
But it helps!
Amazement always helps.
Amazement,
    like awe,
    like reverence,
sharpens the eye,
keens the ear,
quickens the step,
strengthens the hands,
gilds the tongue.

So you must know
those women weren't quiet
for long.
What about you?

Baptized, inundated, flooded
with life.
What about you?
Christened and set ablaze.
What about you?
Nourished and fed.
What about you?

Can you be quiet for long?
Throw off that pall of snow,
that shawl of ice.
Leave behind that winter of silence,
that mute frustration of fear.
Leave it behind.
Come into Easter.
Come into Life.
Light the Fire.
Bake the Bread.
Roast the Lamb.
Come into Life.

Tell someone, anyone, everyone.
Christ is risen
and more.
Christ is risen
and more.

WE BECOME CHRISTMAS (1994)

The liturgical seasons
bind-up my life
in neat parcels
that I carry from month to month.
The climate conforms to my expectations
as it gets dreary during Lent
rains on Good Friday
shines on Easter...
You know what I mean:
cold blasts during Advent
and snow on Christmas.
But not this year.
Advent came in on a Gulf breeze,
not a snowflake lingering
outside any window.
(Checked them all.)
Only the Canada geese were faithful.
They came gaggling out of the north
flapping and honking
shearing the sky's light
with the determined passage
to those southern lakes
and sunny days
locked in the heart's compass.
Like seasoned seamstresses
they stitched their escape
across the garment of sky.
And I wondered why
our passage isn't as firm
as sure
as we darn and mend our way along
the fabric of our journey.

I wasn't expecting it when Jeremiah whispered:
"The days are coming (says the Lord)
when I will fulfill the promise I made..."
Then Baruch chimed in:
"Take off your shoes of mourning and misery
and put on the splendor of glory from God forever."

By now it was the third Sunday
and I was in the mood,
just in time to hear Zephaniah proclaim:
"Shout for joy...sing joyfully, O Israel..."
So when Micah concluded by assuring us:
"His greatness shall reach the ends of the earth.
He shall be peace,"
it was comforting to know
the Lord's plan is not temperature controlled.
The prophets never let us down.
Human life is woven into the divine tapestry
by surer hands than ours.
And all the while
the gospels bore their way into my life
exactly as they told me
the Just Word would do
if only I opened my heart to its fiery call.
But I found myself bound and gagged
with things to say
but no voice to bear the burden.
My little TV screen was a test pattern.
No movement.
No words.
But there are other ways.
So I listened, looking
for the connectedness to Christmas
that would keep me safe.

"Be on guard,"
said Luke,
"lest your spirits become bloated."
But there were Christmas cards to send.
Didn't he know that?
Didn't he have a list?
Yet he didn't give up.
And the second week
Luke shot John
from the canon of Scripture.
"Make ready the way of the Lord."
What did he think I was doing?
Gifts to wrap and all.

But Luke persisted,
"Give your coat away…
share your food…
be content."
Is that what we need to hear?
Now my blood was pumping.
It really was there
all the while
in the blood.
The Word was there.
Then suddenly she came
trudging over the hills
looking for her cousin.
I wait for her each year
but am always stunned when she appears.
Wiry, determined, strong,
smiling, shining, energized,
formidable, uncompromising, committed.
That's what trusting in the Lord
will get you.
And I wondered if the people
I cared about knew.
Did someone tell them?
Had they listened?
Did it matter?
And it all doesn't depend
on the temperature outside
but the fire within.

Then the old nostalgia erupted.
Christmases come and go.
The cookies get baked
even if by different hands.
The tree goes up
although by another's design.
Changing smiles around the table
of our dreams.
But maybe the house still smells like fish
(in my mind at least).
That old ornament emerges each year
and someone still hates fruitcake.
Some are gone from the landscape forever.
And I cried.

But new faces appear.
Hearts bend and lean
with the weight of love.
Sometimes they break
causing us to carry our scars
along with the Magi's gifts
to a child's side.
And he changes with us too.
Full stature,
gentle, prodding.
Severe demands.

We come always again to Christmas
hanging our hopes
on a star of such magnitude and brightness
that everything else
pales in its luster.
But we take on a brilliance,
we become Christmas...
no...Christ
to anyone we care to touch.

THE PAIN OF LIFE (1995)

The pain of life
becomes a companion
a friend we know
a love we embrace.

The tears we cry
water the soul now
and give birth
to our own dying.

We'll know joy
we all see happiness
but these are fleeting
a respite at most.

But the pain of life...

We measure our gains
we count our losses
we fire our dreams
we embrace dashed hopes.

The lives we love
wash over and drench us
like crystal clear water
that dries and disappears.

But in that shower
and in that cleansing
we learn to embrace
our own dying.

The pain of life...

WALKING IN THE WOODS (April 12, 1995)

When the rain cleared
and the sky brightened
I walked the woods
that protect my soul.
    The same old route
    but always new
    and full of surprises.
I gathered up a few stalks
of sunshine.
They actually blazed through the woods
like a laser in my hand.
A few were left behind
so that even in the night
these woods will know some brightness.
And then, there
where I always walk
I spied an old foundation,
some stumbled beams and rotting wood
but beautiful large stones,
ten or twelve at most
forming what used to be
an old entrance, I'm sure.
I've been looking
for these stones.
They will do nicely
for an herb garden,
a raised bed I can work well.
And there was more:
patches of small green shoots
that will be daylilies.
I've never seen them before.
How could I miss them?
Are they so hidden
by summer growth?
I will watch for them now.
And all this was done
and forgotten
by a man who is himself
forgotten or worse,
never known by me.

And someday another
will walk these woods
—I hope—
and wonder
who cut the trails,
who planted the daffodils?
What crazy fool
put tulips in the woods?
And in the questions
I will indeed be remembered
even if never known.
And I will live here forever
because the briars and trees
the blades of grass
the sod and rocks and old pines
have taken in the smell of me
have felt the heaviness of my foot
have absorbed the sweat of my body.
I know well that these woods
do not belong to me,
rather I belong to them.
I do not own this land
nearly as much as it owns me.
And so it will keep me.

*(This poem was read at Joe's burial at the edge of the woods he loved so
well and knew would "keep" him.)*

WHO COULD HAVE IMAGINED IT? (Easter, 1996)

All that creation!
Who could have imagined it?
Darkness and light,
a moon and stars
flung into the abyss.
A sun shining.
Water flowing and
islands of earth
surging to the surface
abounding with life.
Who could have imagined it?
Chaos to creation,
an ongoing process
set into motion
for no other reason than love.
And the capstone gift,
the capstone,
incredible and unthinkable:
male and female in God's image.
And it is all good.
It is all benediction.
Who could have imagined it?
But then the mirror was smudged,
smeared and darkened
by the very ones who could
name it all.
An earth-shattering "NO"
was screamed into existence
by those with power to create,
by those who give ear to the Liar.
They had the shade of the tree of life
and they chose the darkness
of the tree of "knowing-it-all."
But alas, there was no fruit that lasts,
only the dried vestiges of a former life.
They had no limits
until they took a bite of the big lie
becoming prisoners
of their own blindness.

They could quietly name all that was good.
They shouted instead all that was evil.
Running from Grace
they were enveloped by nothingness.
How could they ever find their way back?
Who could have imagined it?

Gifted again
our ancestors discovered
they could embrace despair
or make a return trip.
If only Someone would come along
who knew the way back.
So they looked and waited and
some days even hoped.
Abraham, Moses, Sara, Ruth
Joseph, Mary.
They looked and waited and hoped.
Generation after generation
passing on the dream.
And their journey was
fraught with dangers, lies and bad odds.
The sea of despair,
teaming and treacherous,
seemed uncrossable.
Our mothers and fathers,
like us,
knew times of loneliness and abandonment,
sickness and pain.
But over the wall of alienation
the One who first loved us
threw a rope
braided with repentance and tenderness,
tied securely to a Covenant
much bigger than our sin.
And the waters of separation
became the waters of cleansing,
rebirth and promise.
Who could have imagined it?

Clutching our gods,
our stomachs aching with emptiness
our hearts hollow and bereft
our throats parched and brittle,
we challenged our God
to penetrate with godly passion
the stone of our indifference.
Who could have imagined it?

Sinful but cherished,
soiled now cleansed,
unfaithful yet loved.
The way home was not a lonely road
but a person, a brother, a friend.
Who could have imagined it?
Jesus, the overwhelming Truth,
casts the big lie
onto the shore of our selfishness
and pulls us
naked and vulnerable
into the water.
Our sputtering silenced,
our flailing stilled,
we are led to awesome depths
only to discover
we can swim,
we can swim.
Jesus makes the unrequired,
free-fall plunge
so we can dive into the ocean
of this Easter night.
Who could have imagined it?

The Risen Lord—
    a trumpet of glory
    blasting our names
    into the vault of heaven.
The Risen Lord—
    an eternal Yes
    silencing the NO
    of our stupidity.

The Risen Lord—
    becoming one of us
    so we can be more like him.
Who could have imagined it?

Now I no longer have to worry.
For when I am old
there will be someone
forever young
who will remember
what I was like
before youth and enthusiasm and vibrancy
flew away
leaving me only with memories
that are inexpressible
and defy communication.
The old and young
the strong and sleek
the feeble and weak
all make the crossing
through the life-giving waters.
And reaching the other side
we find a Table set.
Drenched in the unfathomable
flood of grace,
glistening with the sweet-smelling
oil of strength,
enlightened by an undying ember
now fired into white heat,
we are nourished, fed and loved.
Who could have imagined it?

KEEPING WATCH (1996)

With low moaning sounds
clinking and banging
chirping and grinding
the equipment began
the slow methodical
easing of the earth
from its settled landscape.
Early in the morning
energetic workers
set about their tasks
to one purpose:
building up a church so
the Church can continue
to build up the City of God.
The piles of dirt
the gravel
the motored monsters
the pipe and poles
the skids and wire
all stand silent each night
witnesses to something
greater than themselves.
Before we knew it
the soft salmon blocks
outshone
the dull cement ones
and gave form and substance
to what we all longed to see.
The sun continued
to shine hot and humid
but a blessing for builders.
"How soon?" people asked
and "Is it big enough?"
they queried.
"What is that wall?"
they wondered.
But each day we
measured and marked
both time and space
rejoicing to be part of
something unmeasurable
and long-awaited.

Outside my window
the morning sun strikes
the pinkish blocks
so vividly
it is like the striking of a bell
that emits not sound
but color
warmth and light.
And now here come
the iron and steel
sailing through the air
conveyed as if by magic.
Now it looks like a church.
And all the while
the block grows
with an energy of its own.
We look through
glassless windows
to something within.
The church taking shape.
The spiritual dressed
in stone and steel.
A self-awareness.
A new image.
What is the feeling
that is mortared
into reality
when what we have
proclaimed
in Word and Sacrament
is now imprinted
on the landscape?
For us nothing is changed
yet everything is different.
What and who we are
is somehow given
a new dimension
as workers
lift block
push sand
pour water
and with seeming
  effortlessness
give shape to our lives.

And the cement!
Oceans of it.
Flowing
settling
being pushed and pulled.
Dozens of feet
sloshing in the folds
of soft mud.
Like children in a mud hole
they laughed and talked
and unselfconsciously
gave shape and stability
to our stance.
When the trucks
had finished their
spinning and mixing
spitting and sliding
the masons
set about the task of giving
closure to our space
so that now
we were a building
with walls and a floor
yawning into the heavens.

Wooden trusses
like billowing sails
filled the sky and gave
more form to our lives.
Angles and openings
projecting themselves
into reality
while workers
clung to the edges
hemming and hammering
our hopes into place.
And when the sky
could no longer drop
unannounced
into the open space
we rejoiced to be
"under roof."
They unrolled the
black licorice-like paper

and spanned the peaks
side to side.
Inside more walls grew
out of the cement floor.
Wood and block
compartmentalized
our space.
Then one day
there they were!
Huge crosses
in the window holes.
Was that planned?
No matter.
They blessed us
by being there.
Then the rain came
and the snow too.
Shingling half done
now iced with snow
like a birthday cake
looking for candles.
But the work continues
each morning.
Now with light.
Now with heat.
Now here they come
with sparkling squares
of plate glass
flying into gaping holes
necklacing the building
like a cutter's diamonds.
I watch it all from my
watchman's perch.
Can it all be happening
so fast?
Is that drywall I see?
Huge sheets
dwarfing the carrier
waltzing over the
snowbound landscape.
The bundled workers
plodding in and out
more determined than the
severe, relentless snow.

129

The cold pierces
but the work progresses.
The interior begins to
take on shape and style.
Talk of sound and music
speakers and wiring
brings the inevitable closer.
Look!
They're digging the font!
A signature piece
no doubt.
And ideas for
flowing leaded glass
circling the people,
embracing them in
water and holiness.
The Communion of Saints
flowing like a river
clear and crystalline
like waves of baptismal
  water
like rainbowed currents
like springs of life
like the font itself
set free from its
granite bonds
and flung into the light.
Font and Windows.
Water and Light.

Naked walls
in one room now dressed
in warm wooden cupboards.
Rich wooden doors
determine out-places
and add character.
Now the ceilings
have been
whipped-creamed into the
  air
textured and layered.
The whole place is
always suffused in light.

There are windows
where only clouds
peer in rendering
a sense of freedom.
The font stands
a mere shell
crying softly
for granite and water.

The big beams blend
beautifully
into the flow of space
whispering
something of our past.
We look around
amazed each day.
The bubbled skylight
is awed by the clouds
and sheds light
even on a grey day.

Today the walls
come to life.
Peach, blue, white.
A bit of the
Amalfi Coast!
And me with no
bougainvillea!
The carpet is
finally unfurled
like a banner underfoot
softening our steps
surrounded by a
rocky-looking
stream of tile in
colors of life
flowing up, down, around.
We begin to envision
what things will be.
On this wall...
On that wall...
In this space...
Over here...

Sanctuary platform
secured by proud workmen
and finished to a soft
liquidy hue
lies in wait for
an altar and ambo.
Then suddenly
taking us by surprise,
the pews march in
forming straight lines
like biblical sentinels
waiting for the dawn.
They planted their feet
firmly in the floor
and ordered us to
be seated!

In every nook and cranny
the work continues.
All the special
spaces and places
that we will need
to do our work
celebrate our lives
proclaim our faith.
Outside the cement trucks
roar again
as ways and walks
are settled securely into
place.

The warm weather
animates the project.
The earth is moved again
and rolled into its
final resting place.

I realize
from my watch
that the work
will never be finished.
Not only because
we talk of trees and tower
courtyards and crosses
but mostly because
we know
that building a church
is more than a
construction project.
It is a way of life.
And we are a
pilgrim people
nomads on a journey.
Although our tents
are firmly fixed
in an earthly spot
we know that this special
"house for the Church"
provides only temporary
 shelter
for believers who embrace
the never-ending project
of building the Kingdom.

(Written during the construction of St. Luke Church)

REFLECTION OF THE COVENANT (Wedding, 1996)

Muses of our salvation
Fates of our life stories
sing of Abraham and Sarah
Isaac and Rebecca
Joseph and Mary
and countless others
who take their places
in that long line
of marriage partners
who are a clear reflection
of the Covenant
between God and his people.

How we are blessed!
  —We children of these unions.
  —We who are given life and love
through this marvelous Sacrament.
These lovers
who pledge body and soul
carry and are carried
in loving hands
that caress and support
that hold tight
and one day must let go.
These lovers are a sign.
More than rings and candles and cups
they are the clearest symbol
flashed out into a fragile world
to sink roots
while continuing to soar
the vaults of love.

Like that famous couple
at Cana in Galilee
they find that
the water of their lives
is turned to rich red wine
for no other reason than their love
and their willingness
to invite the Lord into their
common life.

Where the wine came from
only they know
and they tell the secret
carefully
in the unfolding of their lives.

QUESTION OF THE HEART (Valentine's Day, 1997)

As we plow and till our way
through the field that is our life
we are often surprised,
taken aback,
when someone is trajectoried
into our landscape.
And more than surprised,
shocked,
to find that they
carve out a place for themselves
in our heart to grow there.
And if,
as we harvest life,
we find that these
lovers and friends leave us,
embracing realities or deaths
we cannot understand,
it is,
once again,
surprising to learn
that the space they have carved,
the furrow where they grew,
remains empty,
yearning,
and is never filled in again.
Holding that emptiness,
we must choose
either to close ourselves off,
leaving behind the planting and gathering
or to make ourselves vulnerable
to new growing,
new entries,
new epiphanies.
It is a question of the heart.

A DIFFERENT ITALY (1997)

This time was different.
Not so much sights
like Rome and Florence.
But a different Italy.
People and faces.
Voices and children.
Food and families.
And scenes
(framed by a train window)
moving by
sometimes slowly
and then in a flash.
Before, Italy impressed me,
thrilled me,
touched me.
This time
I touched Italy.
Face to face,
hand to hand.
The soles of my feet
pressed into her surface.
I could feel her breathing.
Sometimes in young and excited
gasps and gulps.
Sometimes in old sighs
and groans.
The whole gamut of life:
babies and old people,
families and solitary figures,
weddings and funerals,
festivals and daily life.
All with the ever-present awareness
that life is a gift,
fragile and vibrant,
mellow and harsh,
never overrated,
not taking itself too seriously
and most certainly
heading somewhere.

AN EVER-PRESENT NOW (Christmas, 1997)

Driving alone and distracted through the Ohio countryside
the road unrolling ahead,
the smell of burning coal fills the car.
An unmistakable scent.
And all of a sudden I am transported back to childhood.
How can that be
that one quick glimpse of something,
a fleeting fragrance,
a passing déjà vu,
recreates our youth or some day gone by,
thought long forgotten?
How can that be?
Those memories,
those remembrances,
those faces?
They are all there locked into our memory.
And the key that opens that lock
is an unexpected moment,
a fleeting sensation.
How can that be?
More incredible still is that in a condensed moment
we can remember huge chunks of our life.
The remembering, itself only a twinkling,
seems to stretch into eternity.
Yet it is only that,
a moment, seconds.
And in that sliver of time we conjure up again
Christmases, trips, reunions,
separations, arguments.
Something that took hours, days, weeks, years,
a whole segment of our lifetime,
is capsulized in a flash.
And we relive it again.
Alas, though memory may comfort us
it cannot give life.
Christmas mandates more than memory.
For it is not a past birth we celebrate
but a present reality, sometimes harsh and harrowing.
I will stand now and sing an elegy
to all the brown grasses and black shrubs
that may wear the ermine cope of wintertime.

For soon they too will be but a memory
when the emeralds and bright jewels of Spring
once again adorn the garment of the earth.
Life is a pilgrimage into the future
not a retreat into the past.
No doubt Mary longed for the days gone by.
You know,
before the angel
before the pregnancy
before the emperor and his decrees.
And what of Joseph?
Didn't he think of those peaceful past days
before the dreams disturbed his soul?
His busy shop, his clothes,
his very face awash in the smell
of cedar, olive wood and sweat.
The peaceful reminiscences of a quiet man.
Even (T.S. Eliot's) magi longed for their
"Summer palaces on slopes, the terraces
and the silken girls bringing sherbet."
Now here they all are,
pilgrims on the road,
displaced, reluctantly tramping out new memories
from a dangerous present
into an uncertain future.
For Mary and Joseph, for the magi,
giving birth to tomorrow depended,
as it does for us all,
on living today with faith.
To us a child is born.
Momentous monosyllables someone called them.
For us, Christmas centers on a Child.
Yesterday's child.
Today's child.
Tomorrow's child.
To forget any is to forget Christmas.
It is true that since that night long ago
our world can never be the same.
Because of Bethlehem's child
no one and nothing can be left untouched.
The Child cannot be
memoried into one Holy night,
hollowed into some nostalgic yesterday.

Keep in mind that there is another holy night
when we keep vigil waiting for the dawn
when the man-child is born again
into what we all must become.
And so Christmas is an ever-present "now."
For us and for God
who not only created space and time
but entered into them
became our flesh and blood,
our kin, our child.
Christmas is a Holy secret
shouted into the darkness
about every mother's child for all time.

THE WOODS TODAY (February 6, 1998)

The woods, indeed
the land and air,
shimmer today
veils of ice clinging to the trees
        —branches and trunks.
Icing like on a cake
extends over the grasses
and ground covers.
Today the woods are silent
so quiet that the very
shimmering
resounds
a quiet chorus.
The sun leaps
from tree to tree.
There is a crust on the quarry.
I dare not walk it.
Plodding along the quarry rim
I thought of Joe
a reverie I have not allowed myself
for some time.
Today the earth enveloped me
and claimed another
inch or two
of my personal landscape
my soul.

A HOUSE IN CALABRIA (August 8, 1998)

Is there a difference
between dreaming
and seeing possibilities?
I hope not.
With an almost crazed tenacity
I convince myself
that I can dream my possibilities
into reality.
Even unfulfilled dreams
change the direction
    —not the destination—
of my life into something
other than it would have been
with no dreaming.
My mental meanderings
about a Calabrian retreat
will either crystallize into reality
or become just a new image
in the present landscape of my mind.

A SEASONAL REMINISCENCE (July 14, 1999)

Already the summer grasses are leaning into August with a maturity
befitting the elderly. I can count over a dozen colors of green in the
silent trees, not even a breeze to give them an attitude adjustment.
The birdbath is dry and hospitality demands I correct that problem.
Else how will the birds know this is their place and I'm just passing
through, intending them no harm?

TIME TO REFLECT (Lake Erie, 1999)

<u>Sunday Evening</u>
Falling out of routine
and into days
without a clock,
I grab hold of my thoughts
and look for insight.

<u>Monday Morning</u>
The sun just spread a blanket
on the long picnic table.
Usually my senses are perched,
ready to pounce,
wanting desperately to be in touch
with anything outside themselves.
Today though
I find myself too willing
to leave my senses behind
and plunge into a pool
of memories
where I can search
not for the security of the past
but for a new direction,
where the ripples on the surface
of the water of my life
will find depth,
even leagues,
into which I can dive for treasure.
Bruce in my CD player
going "down to the river."
Everyone is looking for something.
Everyone has losses to recoup
and promises to keep
and hopes to fulfill.

<u>Friday Morning</u>
The trains whistle their way
into my room
and from my bed
        —like a depression-displaced hobo—
I hitch a ride.
The trains don't so much keep me awake
as carry me through the night.

Wheels whine and whistles whirl
through the darkness
only the engineer can trust.
I wonder if there are still
car repairmen
who lie on their backs
in cold damp places
notching and twisting
stubborn steel into safe joints.
I wonder if they are still there.
And do wives and children
still get free passes
to exotic places like
Philadelphia and Chicago,
New York and Niagara Falls,
where they can be charmed
entertained and sustained even
by busy streets and backstairs,
fresh fish and bakeries,
neighborhood bars,
and Aunt Annie's
cornflakes and grapefruit juice
that always tasted better than home?
Or has all that
been Disneyed away
never to thrill again
except in memory
when train whistles blow
and the sun stays
considerately hidden
until the daydreams of night
are complete?

Tuesday Morning
An almost imperceptible rain
is silking and silting
through the crisp air.
Autumnal preview no doubt.
No siren call to the beach today.
A week ago it was 100 degrees!
Another time.
Another place.
Another life maybe.

THIS BIRTH (Christmas, 1999)

With an aching purity
unknown on the earth
the seamless robe of this holy night
lays itself firmly
upon the shuddering shoulders
of the hesitant world
and engulfs us
in an expansive coverlet
of passion love and forgiveness.
The geography of the planet
is hardly moved.
But Oh, the spiritual landscape
is shaken earthquaked
into new shapes
as the inbreak of God thunders and rolls
out of the Eastern horizon.

Now the tramping boots of bloody battle
are given a name
and it is SIN.
Now the heartless ravages of poverty
are seen in the light
and they are INJUSTICE.
Now the cold and closed
unforgiving hearts
have a new identity
and it is UGLINESS.
Now the thrones of power and selfishness
are seen in all their stark NOTHINGNESS.

For now,
with our *Fiat*
Grace
Justice
Beauty and
Abundance
can circle the fractured globe
with mending sheets
drenched in the healing balm of Gilead.

It is to the hollow human eye
an unremarkable birth
humble sparse even unnecessary.
A birth plagued by the homelessness
that will always stalk the earth.
A birth threatened by the demons
that create widows and orphans
tears and sadness.
The demons that make death an enemy
rather than a homecoming.
But make no mistake
it is a birth of light
for those who would rub their eyes
and look again.
A birth of wonder and hope
for gentle hearts that would know
the awesome presence of God
and the unrelenting power
of forgiveness and mercy.

This birth will not take away
the emptiness
ushered in by friendship lost
but will give us a companion
to walk the heart's journey.

This birth will not fill the chair
that cradles grief
over the one newly departed from us.
Nor does it take the place of the one
still sorely missed
after so many years.
But this birth will give us a dinner guest
who brings the bread for the feast
where all are alive.

Shepherds and swaddling clothes
Angels and Kings
are firmaments of faith
not to be found
on the dusty pages
of history books.

These realities
appear only to the eyes of children
and those who would lay
aside the deceiving sophistication
of human perception.
It is indeed a Silent Night
for it is only in Silence that words
gain meaning.

There are no burdens too heavy
for this birth to bear.
Yet we lay upon it
the wrong baggage
that doesn't need to be carried anywhere.

This birth cannot meet
the insatiable debilitating cravings
that we nourish and fondle
but it can addle the addictions
we will to overcome
leaving them to their own destruction.

This birth will not disappear the hurts
that we give and receive
but it will ferment the wine of forgiveness
we can pour into one another's wounded hearts.

Again
we come
a long line of sinners and saints
gazing out into the moonlit
vault of sky.
We entertain a daring dream.
We juggle expectant hopes.
We gaze into the inky liquid darkness.
WE look for a new day.
YOU step to the window.
I take my place next to you.
And we are not alone.
Like Magi
the stars sing on the windowpane
and wait for the morning light.

REMEMBERING JOE: "<u>The</u> Father Joe Fata"

I will never forget the tall priest who had a certain swagger about him as well as a genuine concern for humanity. Our bond developed when the Union Church and I became a part of ACTION. We challenged each other, respected each other, and loved each other. That relationship grew to the point that I brought him to the Union Church one Sunday morning to preach to our congregation. There was great hesitation from congregants, as well as doctrinal difference, but the one common thread that ran through us despite our differences was Christ. When he finished his presentation the church erupted and wanted to know when he would be back again. So too it was when we came to St. Luke and the unknown was written on many faces; but when the Lord had done His perfect work, they too learned the power of the "AMEN" LOL! He believed what he believed and served to the fullest of his capacity, and for this he will forever be etched in my mind and in my heart. Rest well my friend, we will meet again. We will meet again!!

—Pastor Michael H Harrison, Sr.

CHAPTER FIVE
ST. LUKE II (2000-2002)

BREAKING HEARTS (2000)

When a heart breaks
it doesn't make a sound for the ear,
not a tinkle or crack.
But the noise it makes
in our brain is deafening.
Likewise it mends
just as quietly
to the ear.
But again
in the mending
it causes great consternation
in the mind.
Tonight I measure my path
and wait for someone to come
quietly
and caress my head,
all the while knowing
it will never happen.
I dip my pen
into the ink of self-awareness
and draw lines over my melancholy.
Or are the lines
in truth
the tracks
that always bring the next train
promising to carry me forward
onward
in this pilgrimage I have chosen?

LENT IN A TIME OF WAR (2000)

When Jesus told the disciple
to sheath his sword and
proceeded to replace the ear
of the high priest's servant,
he made it clear that violence
can never be used in the name
of religion,
or even in the name of faithfulness to him.

And now we,
frightened children of the mean centuries,
continue swiping and slashing
at the ears of enemies unknown and unnamed.

How can we preach the Word
with blood on our mouths?
How can we speak to our young
of traditions and faith
when they come home in body bags
surrounded by the sounds of missiles and guns?

How can we sing Amazing Grace
to severed ears that cannot hear?
How can we speak words of love
to hearts that have been riddled by bullets?

When the full moon of Lent
peers into my window at night
flooding my space with a mythic light
that would shed peace on a fractured world,
I shut my eyes (tight)
to maintain the darkness.
I do not see the bodies of the children.
I do not look at the blood on my windowpane.
I do not imagine the Christ on the Cross.
No, I think of my sacrifice in giving up chocolate
and sleep fitfully.

MOM'S DISH (2000)

It's not a spectacular dish,
simple really,
cut glass
rectangular
8 x 5.
But it was her dish.
A wedding gift maybe
from a simpler day,
I don't know.
For me it is an anchor
mooring me to my mythical past.

I can see it in our dining room
on table or buffet.
If stored,
always in reach
for cranberries at Thanksgiving
or colored eggs at Easter.
Now with maple crèmes
    pilfered from Dad's hiding place,
    proffered for all.
Now with Annaclairs,
    those creamy peanut clusters
    that appeared mysteriously.
Once, I remember, with Jell-O.

I use it now.
It helps me hear the sunrise
or settle an argument.
It is a small parcel of peace
in a convoluted world.
"You shouldn't use it,"
someone said.
"What if it breaks?"

If it breaks and dies
as we all must,
then it had a life
that can be celebrated
and remembered.

And now I have
crafted these words
so that when the dish
or I
are gone
the words will give it memory.
Now if it shatters
it can take its place
among the crystal stars
secure in all it has held.

IN PUGLIA (September 18, 2000)

From where I stand,
on the beach in Puglia,
looking toward Calabria
I can see the sun sinking
into the western line.
The sunpath on the water
is like Dorothy's
yellow brick road,
     rippling and undulating,
     shining and gleaming,
that could take me to another place,
a place of fancy or dreams,
a place of hope or desire.
Or it could just take me home
to Calabria.

ON THE TRAIN TO MILAN (September 25, 2000)

A passing panorama.
Italy unfolded,
discovered,
yet hidden,
always ready to reveal
something new.
Here a different story
than the one in the South,
told by shepherds
and olive groves,
caverns and coastlines.
Italy,
like an unfaithful lover
kisses both
Adriatic and Mediterranean
with equal passion.
But the heart of Italy
remains true to itself
so that every lover
can carve out a space
and be embraced,
convinced that
Italy is his alone, hers only.
And it is so.

OCTOBER SUN (October 27, 2000)

October sun,
a bonus blessing
for people anticipating
the lips of winter
kissing our warmth goodbye.
Today the boring household chores accomplished
I allow myself a brief walk
looking for bittersweet
and pods
gifts of Autumn
and promise of winter.

SEND THOSE ANGELS (Christmas, 2000)

Those angels!
Those apocalyptic angels!
Those soaring, penetrating angels!
The angel that flashed into
the lives of quiet, fleecy shepherds,
and then that multitude,
fleet and sure,
that fired the night sky
over Bethlehem.
Were they all herald angels
or did some have other occupations?
Have you ever thought about it before?

Of course you expect herald angels
at Christmas,
even though nobody "harks" anymore.
I knew
there would be heralding angels
when this galloping year
came charging headlong
out of the millennium horizon.
I had grown accustomed to herald angels,
had seen them before,
heard their song,
felt the beat of their wings
on the drum of my soul.
At least I thought they were herald angels.
Now I am not so sure.
After all, what is a herald angel anyway?

When Gabriel appeared to Mary
to herald her future
he was first a comforting angel.
"Do not be afraid, Mary."
Maybe he was a comforting angel
who did some
heralding on the side.
Even the shepherds
had to be calmed before they could hear.
"Do not be afraid, Shepherds."
Heralding is only part of it.

And what about old Zechariah,
when he discovered that his
aging, loving Elizabeth
carried a belly full of the Baptist?
Gabriel, who certainly had some news for him
had to shut the old man up
so he would know it was
serious business,
this procuring of a Savior.
A silencing angel no doubt.

And don't forget dreamy Joseph.
Do you wonder why
he ever went to bed?
Every time he nodded off
another angel
mushroomed into his sleepy head.
Another angel
straight from the "Jobs R Us" department
with another challenge to face,
another trip to make,
another problem to solve,
another threat to stare down.
He got more than sleep or good news
in those midnight meanderings.
It's enough to make one
an insomniac.

O yes,
there are lots of angel episodes
peppered throughout our great story.
And they are not merely herald angels.

So now I'm convinced
heralding is only part-time work.
And this year I know for sure,
because
I have encountered other angels,
and so have you.

The Angel Muse
makes space in our cob-webby minds
and hollow hearts
so we can
find sonorous words,
discover piercing prayers,
see vibrating images
and ultimately
prepare a secure place
where God's glory
can indeed be kindled.

The Angel Portal
is a wide door through which
we first can see
and then walk
to encounter the God
who always has a plan
even if we don't like it.

The Angel Guide
is the traveling companion
who offers a steady hand,
and sometimes carries us
over those treacherous trails
and threatening trials
that blacken our hillside
so we cannot see the clarion stars
that shimmer in our hearts.

And don't forget
the Strong Angel, Michael
and his friendly cohorts,
who can make devils
tremble and tumble.
The angel of Strength
who can get inside us
and find
and push
to the top
the will to fight,
the muscle we need,
the courage we didn't know we had.

O yes,
and remember
the Healing Angel
who brings cure or calm,
whichever is best for us.
That angel of mercy
who can root out sickness or sin,
who can find health and wholeness
deep within the most
battered body or abused soul.

How wonderful to have a God
Who cannot be contained in God-self
but must create angelic realities
to proffer his presence,
to transport his grace,
to fly into our sky.

How wonderful to have a God
Who loved us enough to become enfleshed
in an ordinary child in the Bethlehem hills.
Who trusted us enough to become
a vulnerable man who walked the Palestine plains.
Who cared enough to climb Golgotha's hill.
Who forgave us enough to become nailed and butchered.
Who was faithful enough to rise from the depths of death itself.
Who will not allow us to mourn forever.

How astounding it is to have a God
Who, not content
with angelic presence or even incarnation,
chooses to become one with each of us
so we can become one with one another.

How incredible it is to have a God
Who becomes both Table companion
and the very food we eat.

How humbling to have a God
Who will stop at nothing
to be with us.

How reassuring to have a God
Who isn't finished yet.

So send those angels.
Heralding,
comforting, calming,
strengthening, silencing angels.
Send those dream angels
and those angels of mercy.
Angels of healing,
angels of magic and mystery,
angels of peace.
Send them in multitudes,
send them in pairs,
send them one at a time.

Send them for a Child
born in a stable rich with love and warmth.
Send them for a Man
who died and rose
so we would know.

Send them for people
scattered over the hillsides of life
but gathered in your name,
people of the promise
always coming true.

VALENTINE'S DAY TO ASH WEDNESDAY (2001)

The revolving earth
turns slowly out of the brilliance
into another night
leaving an aurora
in my sky
in my eye.
Rough-edged pilgrims
we punctuate our wandering
only now and then
to roll up warmly
into a blanket stitched
from dreamy days
or restless nights.

We rush from
hearts to ashes
desperately seeking love.

INVITATION AND LIFE (Easter, 2001)

I think that only doubters and non-believers
look for an empty tomb.
It's the proof they need to contain the miracle
and keep it at a distance.
Me, I want my tombs to be full and threatening.
Full of angels, full of light, full of life, full of demands.
At the gaping door of death,
the women found
not emptiness, but fullness,
more than they had hoped for.
Who has not stood at the grave of a loved one
wanting desperately to see more than stone and dirt?
Who has not learned, like the women at the tomb,
that our burial rituals are empty gestures
when there is no hope?
They found that the damned door to that tomb
was the delightful door to their future.
It required something of them.
Isn't it strange,
although the men dismissed their story as nonsense
they went to see anyway?
As though the emptiness could be more convincing
than woman's word and woman's experience.
Maybe they couldn't admit that the women were on to something,
something their dullness dare not dream.
Or maybe they didn't realize
their loneliness and hunger
had opened them to amazement.
Certainly Peter's betrayal
disposed him to the women's truth,
made him realize his need for other believers,
made him understand
that alone, one cannot follow Christ.
He ran to see.
And so did the others.
The Gospels don't tell us everything.
I'll bet every one of his followers
went to check out that burial ground.
What were they looking for?
They were looking for Easter!
It just didn't have a name yet.

They were looking, like you and me,
for signs of hope and a life to lean on.

On Holy Thursday
when we washed one another's feet,
we knew death could not hold one who loves that much.
We knew his command to bow before one another
was not a mere mandate but a living word
or a word to live by,
a word that frees us from death.

On Good Friday,
when the cross brushed our fingers and we wept,
when our lips touched the wood and we winced,
we knew in our heart of hearts
that death could not hold him who died for life.

We knew. We knew.
But we run to see for ourselves too.
We know that Christian faith
does not teeter on an empty tomb
but rests on the experience of the Risen One.
And the fact that
Resurrection faith shares space
with the horrible memory of
sin, betrayal, crucifixion and death
only makes it more precious.
It is no accident that there is no description of the Resurrection,
no blow by blow account of the event.
All the Scriptures give us is the before and the after.
Otherwise, we would be like the two-year-old
looking at an ancient family photo
and asking: where was I?
No this story must leave room for everyone.
Everyone is in the picture
—a picture in process—
because the Kingdom of God
is not merely about words and ideas,
it is about a way of life.
The Easter Story is all we have.
But don't be fooled.
It is enough to fight off sickness and death.

Evil is powerful
but it cannot stand up to our Story.
Our story is not merely told,
it is lived and loved.
It is a trumpet in the heart
that sounds a clarion call into a hardened world.
It is a clashing symbol that reverberates
through all our grief, our joyless days
our dejections and death.
Some nights last until dawn.
But even a dark and desolate landscape
can be illuminated by an Easter story moon
until the sun has time to rise and warm the face again.
One poet says that the Easter Story teaches us to dream,
teaches us to live threatened by Resurrection.
It is a threat to the sinful security we think we like.
So go to the tomb if you will,
stoop down,
peer in,
don't be afraid.

It won't be empty.
It will be full of invitation and life.
It will be overflowing with news for you to tell.

IN THE WOODS (May 3, 2001)

Every trail was hung thick
with the fragrance of Autumn Olive.
The sweet pungent smell
cascaded off the tree limbs,
swelled out of the earth
and assaulted every breath.
The hillsides and paths
danced and sparkled
with a full cast of characters:
Trillium—white, pink and red
Violets—purple, white and yellow
Spring Beauties and Bluets
Wild Geraniums, cinque foil
and uncounted, unnamed blossoms,
no less beautiful
because of my lack of acquaintance.
A deer bounded away
across the princess pine
and a turkey gobbled in the distance,
too shrewd to be seen by me.

I moved as if in a fantasy world
unhampered by what
Gerard Manley Hopkins
would call
man's smudge.
It was a brief respite
but enough to revitalize,
enough to lure me back again.

Call to ACTION (May 29, 2001)

You and I
meager
sometimes pathetic
human beings try
to capture the Great Mystery
to contain the All-Powerful
to possess the All-Loving.
We give this great "I AM"
our handy names:
God
Allah
Elohim
Yahweh
Khuda
Yazdan
Tanri
Theos
Deus
Abba.
We think that
by naming
in praying
even in loving
we can somehow own
the Magnificent Other
who is the ground of our being.
We easily forget the important truth:
that this Tremendous Lover
has first loved us;
that this Great Unnameable
has first named us;
that this wonderful "object" of Faith
has first, Faith in us.
And so we gather
to lay claim to our birthright
to proclaim the truth
to celebrate the reality.
A wise Hasidic insight
reveals that in the palace of the King
there are many rooms
and there is a key for each one.

An axe is however
the pass-key of all pass-keys.
For with it
one can break through all the doors and gates.
Each prayer has its own proper meaning
and is therefore
the specific key
to a door in the Divine palace.
But a broken heart
is an axe which opens all the gates.
And so I'm thinking:
Division breaks our hearts
but it will not crush our spirit of unity.
Separation breaks our hearts
but it will not quell the desire for connectedness.
Isolation breaks our hearts
but it will not keep us from building bridges.
Dishonesty breaks our hearts
but it will not extinguish the flame of integrity.
Corruption breaks our hearts
but it will not quench our thirst for justice.

So here we come.
Count us,
broken-hearted children
of the wicked years.
Here we come
with our hopes.
Here we come
holding pieces
of one another's hearts
in trembling hands.
Here we come
tired and weak
but ready to take ACTION.
Indeed, with the axe of a broken heart
we will break down the barriers
        we will throw open the gates
            we will unlock the doors
                we will stand before our God
no matter the name
and we will not be spurned.

We would take back
our neighborhoods
our cities
our towns
our lives.
O yes, we will take back
all that has been wrested from our hands.

We will also take back
that which we foolishly handed over through
stupidity
apathy
selfishness and greed.
We will reach far and wide.
We will pull together all that has been ripped apart.
We will not be separated
by imaginary lines
created by others
and laid down on maps
which we never asked to be drawn.
We will not submit to schemes
meant to dupe us into lethargy.
We will not accept leadership
placed by its own arrogance.
We will not forget our dreams.
We will not lose hope.

For we will be tailors and seamstresses
    of a new fabric
woven by faith and hard work
    of a new garment
worn in dignity and pride
    of a new government
where no one will ever say again
"That's the way it is"
    of a new community
where children will be honored and formed
as gifts for our future
    of a new society
where oppression and poverty
are words in a history book
    of a new world
where all people can call freely to their God.

And finally then
this great Mending God
will take up the needle with us
and stitch together
even our broken hearts.

LAKE ERIE (July 27, 2001)

A typical Lake Erie gale
has been growling out of Canada.
The Lake has oceaned
into huge waves
that roll and roil and toss
the gleeful kids around
like beach balls.
Even the sand is Saharaed
and rippled into a dry ocean
of granulated waves and dunes.
I sit on my blanket oasis,
my back needled and acupunctured
by the blowing grit.
It is not unpleasant,
rather invigorating.
So we are back.
Another year punctuated
by lazy lake days.

ON THE LAKE (August 31, 2001)

On the Lake
I float out of my own prison
into a freedom
that speaks clearly
of sun and sand
water and dreams.
The envelope of earth
that holds me
is more than a life raft.
It is a spirit-filled place
of memories and stone,
of past and present and future.
Then I raise
the sails of the seasons
and crest into tomorrow.
But it is always
the experience
of latching onto,
of leashing
a memory
and walking it around a bit
that sets the creative juices
flowing.
I know, of course,
my expression,
my words,
are inept
and never quite contain
the richness of the reverie
or the substance of the thought.
But then
I am like most,
more than any of us pretend to be,
searching as we do
for uniqueness
when it is really commonality
we desperately seek.

THE CHRISTMAS PROMISE (2001)

The year seemed to
drizzle into a damp and dreary demise.
Our "old heavens" have
certainly left us.
Now we have no choice
but to be open to new
advances and adventures
from a God with
marvelous plans for the future.
Our God will NOT dwell on
bad thoughts and grudging memories
    tear filled images of death
        or losses that leave us limp and shaking.

So what did you get for Christmas?
A miracle maiden,
indeed mild
but not too.
Strong enough to say yes to God.
That's what we needed.
That's what we got.

But that's not all.
We got a reminder of what we can be,
we who have been
September eleventhed into reality.
A reminder of what we can do,
we who have been shaken
by ultimate calamities
or bent by private pain
and emerged
not by our own power
but by the compassion of God.
    Emerged on the wings of angels.
        Emerged with the prayers of the saints.

Emerged with the knowledge
the awareness
the conviction
that those who look to the Lord
will know peace
even if
terrorized and hounded
by evil from without
or sin from within.
They can
hate us off the face of the earth
but they can never leave us
bereft, broken or empty
now that we are one with God
because God chose to be one with us.

So what did you get for Christmas?
The Christmas story.
The Christmas promise.

A strong woman, a worried man,
a baby and shepherds and wise men
are just the beginning.
And the gift is Christmas itself
that lets us say "yes" to God
and make it more than resignation.
It is the gift of reminding us that,
like a pilgrim Mary
carrying a baby in her belly
or a displaced Joseph
with a dream in his heart
we too can travel
a confused and winding road
to even a closed door
and still not be without a heart to sleep in.

What did you get for Christmas?
The power to move
with grace through this trembling world
with faith and not a small amount of hope.

Even in our poverty we discover
enough to sustain ourselves
and any who do not possess
whatever it takes to know God.
Angels aren't the only heralds.

Christmas itself is the gift
no, the promise
that cascades from
the whispering hills of Bethlehem
into the scattered centuries...
the promise
that the voices of those
who cry in the wilderness
        will never be outshouted by screams of hatred
        will never be buried by whispers of apathy.

What did you get for Christmas?
The assuaging assurance that
explosions of terror
and even death planes
cannot silence
the thunder of Glory
that rolls from the heavens
in the Angels' song
of peace on earth
to people whose will is
right and good,
to people whose heroism
burns brighter than any fire.

What did you get for Christmas?
The discovery that
we can do more
than shake our fists
at what we cannot control
because after generations of relentless
envoys
God himself came
in the heart of one small woman
to make sure we get the point.

The light from one dancing star
can bring kings out from their pleasure domes
and shepherds in from their fields.
The Light from one virgin heart
can shine in the crevices
of the most exhausted soul
and coax it into life.

So what did you get for Christmas?

From MYSTERY (Easter, 2002)

Blustering and tenacious,
a schizophrenic March
plucked us by the nape of the neck
to shake us into April.
Tired but relieved,
we look to the sky searching
for the sunrays that
will warm our waffling spirits.
Hopeful and willing,
we look to the earth
for signs of green and
even small explosions of color.
It doesn't take much to encourage us
to drop the wraps of winter
and with naked, Lenten, shriven spirits
embrace the joyful
yet terrible meaning of Easter.

Incredible
that the fire pot of one Easter night
can melt the snows of bad memories
along with
the icy shards of sin that
pin us to our pathetic past.
It flickers and flames
dances and darts,
that fire.
And it whispers to us,
"step inside, step inside."
And like brave and sure
Joan of Arc,
we Easter people embrace the flames
and discover a cool grace.
Then, still red and ruddy
from the fire's heavenly heat
we jump headlong into the Waters of New Life.

We are indeed,
a church of extremes,
a community of overstatement,
people of abundance
      —when it comes to holiness and wholeness
      you can never get too much of a good thing.
The fire is never bright enough.
The water is never deep enough.
The oil is never flowing enough.
The bread and wine are never abundant enough
to portray the wide, unfathomable truths
they sacramentalize.
They are human elements
after all
that force us to rely on
Mystery
to accomplish the impossible.
Mystery—with arms expansive enough to embrace a weary world.
Mystery—with a heart big enough to include every culture.
Mystery—with feet sure enough to walk the most challenging road.
Mystery—with shoulders broad enough to carry the weight of the
sinful centuries.
Mystery—with light bright enough to change the most entrenched
and arrogant mind.
Mystery—with faith deep enough to admit wrongs and bring a
healing balm from Gilead to sooth the troubled waters of the human
sea.
Refreshed is not good enough!
We are REBORN in the waters of Baptism,
rising to new and everlasting life.

ABUNDANCE AND BLESSING (Wedding, 2002)

The bride and groom at Cana
had to know there was more to life
than a jug full of wine.
Yet, the symbol remains deep and abiding,
overflowing with life and love.
They had to know
somewhere deep in their bones
that the presence of Christ
would bring to their lives
a richness unfathomed
by so many others
who enter into marriage
that is more like
a business agreement than a love affair,
more like a cheap romance novel
than golden poetry and singable prose.
They had to know their love
was thicker than water.
And so they invited
Jesus
to the celebration
setting the stage for more than one miracle.
Some scholars tell us his apostles drank too much.
Maybe Mary really said
"Your 12 friends drank up all the wine;
now fix it!"
But Jesus is always about
Abundance and Blessing.
And so...
surrounded by family and friends
that Cana couple
was launched into a life of love
by the one who moves marriage
from mere romance to
a life of commitment, unselfishness and dedication.

Today this bride and groom
have come to this holy place,
this place of memory and hope,
this holy ground
where they can be connected
to births and baptisms,
communions and confirmations,
marriages,
yes and even the deaths
of those loving ghosts
who have gone before them,
who are with them still,
who, over the years
have pressed the grapes of life
to prepare the wine
that Jesus will pour into their hearts today.
For this bride and groom also
have invited Jesus to the celebration.
And they have invited us,
we who love them
and tender them
into a hopeful future flowing
with wedding day wine.
It is fitting for us to be here,
for it is a future we walk together.
We are of a piece you know.
No marriage is lived in isolation
once it has been named a Sacrament,
once it has been blessed by the miracle of flowing wine,
once it has been tied to the threads
of yesterday
and knitted into the fabric of tomorrow.
It is true
that today these two
become a Sacrament,
a sign,
a promise
to the worried fragile world.
We are witnesses to this Sacrament-making,
this fermenting of grapes,
this wine-making day,
this time of rich wine poured out.

And we will never look at them
in the same way again.
For they will be
a sacrament of God's love,
a sign of Christ's presence,
a promise to carry us all into tomorrow.

PUGLIA: THE LONGING (April, 2002)

*(The Gargano Peninsula is lovely and Vieste is a scenic town cut into the
sea rock. The view out our hotel window is breathtaking.)*

I dream today
of another mythic Pugliese sunset.
Only it is September
and that Adriatic sun shakes
his dependable golden locks
burning the sea water,
searing my soul.
Yet it was the other coast
that I longed for then
and still now.
  The cousins who warm my heart
  more than the Calabrian skies.
  The father whose footsteps
  I would trace
  even though they never
  left imprints in the sand.
  It is another mark he made
  and I am not the only one touched by it.

TO HOLD A PIECE OF THE EARTH (2002)

I am thinking today
of the kind and thoughtful
man at the engineer's office.
He sent me maps
—free of charge—
of our little piece of Hope
in Elkrun Township.
It occurred to me
as I held the map
over against the vastness
of God's great earth
—it occurred to me—
how foolish seem
our pathetic little parcels
of land
which we pretend to own
and improve.
We speak of buying and selling,
ingress and egress,
permanent and temporary,
yours and mine,
his and ours,
hers and theirs.
All the while
missing the heart of the matter
as we, in our frenzy,
only obliquely touch
the good earth
that would, indeed,
hold us in a more permanent embrace
if we would but open our hearts.

It is a dream,
I know,
to think it could be otherwise.
But then
what is there to sustain us
if not our dreams.

To hold a piece of the earth
in trust,
in common,
indeed
is but the waking dream
of poets and philosophers
and poor men and women
who know well
what each hand can hold
and that no hand holds enough.
And so it becomes a dream
of touching hearts as well as soil,
of holding hopes as well as documents,
of reaching for stars as well as titles.
I think then
the place to call our own
is at best a symbol,
a paradigm,
for belonging
for being held
for being owned
—in fact—
by someplace
    something
        someone
greater than ourselves,
greater even than our dreams.

LOOKING ALWAYS FOR THE THANKFUL HEART
(Thanksgiving, 2002)   A Reflection on Luke 17:11-19

And the Samaritan said:
Forgive them Lord
for healing is truly a frightening thing.
Our sickness gives us identity.
It provides comfort
when we have nothing else
to cling to.
It can be a safe haven
from the awesome voice of God.
Thanksgiving is hard
for one who considers himself
burdened.
It is impossible for one without faith.
And remember Lord,
it takes great faith to see
that Night grows
timidly
out of the fading light.
And, as it grows,
it envelopes us
in an ominous blackness
in which the Voice of God
can be *heard
and indeed *seen
for what it is:
*a calming whisper
*a shimmering light.
Forgive them Lord.
They don't know
there is a fiery flash
on the other side of darkness,
a rolling thunder
on the other side of silence.
If we would
see the flash and hear the roar
of God's love,
we must embrace the silence
and kiss the darkness
and only then comes
the heart able to offer thanks.

Yet even a thankful heart is your gift.
So forgive them Lord.
And me...
Keep me in such a way
that
filled with hope
and armed with the
sharp silver knife of faith
I may cut a slice of life each day
—a slice just large enough
to share
but small enough
to carry unencumbered
through a world
glutted with its own fullness
and sated with selfishness
beyond humanity.
Keep me Lord
among the thankful ones
even the poor ones.
The ones who come back
not because they are satisfied
but because they are hungry.
Hungry for healing
and looking always for
the thankful heart.

REMEMBERING JOE: "Part of Something Bigger"

Every book has a purpose. Although I never had the opportunity to discuss the purpose of this book with Father Fata directly, I believe I experienced it instead. One of those evenings of poetry reading proved to be an extra special event, one of the many gifts that were at first disguised by sadness, tears and anticipated loss. He would pick who would read which poem. I can close my eyes and see him handing me "An After Easter Diary." As I began reading, I was transported back to April 11, 1998 and that miraculous Easter Vigil when I experienced my own initiation into the church. The sights, sounds and smells of that solemn night came alive again for me, even though it was so many years ago. It was only the taste of my tears that brought me back to the room. Looking at Father Fata, I saw more than just tears in his eyes. I saw a little amazement, perhaps wondering how his words could do this. Then as I finished, he gave a subtle smile and nod of his head as we all agreed this poem should be included.

I am blessed to have known Father Fata for 19 years. A gifted artist, poet, homilist, and of course Pastor and friend, his words have touched and encouraged many. He has always inspired us to share our talents to benefit others. With these poems he opens his soul and continues to teach, inspire and even take us back to memories that perhaps need revisiting.

What is the purpose of this book? Don't be mistaken into thinking it is about the life of a priest! It is about seeing God in the ordinary and in the beauty of nature. It is about traditions and relationships with each other and with Jesus. It is about being open to the power of the Holy Spirit and how to build a better church for a better tomorrow. The purpose is to challenge us to remember that we are children of God, to love God and neighbor, and to celebrate that we are part of something bigger.

—Theresa Marx-Armile

CHAPTER SIX
ST. LUKE III (2003-2008)

MIRACLE AND MYSTERY (Easter, 2003)

(Note: I have always believed that there are times and events when ordinary, everyday language just does not capture the experience. So once again, for this great expansive feast of Easter, the greatest feast of the Church Year, I share my words and images.)

Miracle and Mystery
always take us by surprise!
Even when we pray for it,
desire it,
hope for it,
we are taken by surprise.
Miracle and Mystery
make us forget
we were ever immersed in
pessimism and doubt.
Miracle and Mystery!
Here it is, all of a piece.
Where once was only droning
now—poetry and song.
Where once was only
our disconsolate desert
now—wondrous water.
Where once was darkness and death
now—blazing light and blossoms afire.
Miracle and Mystery!

Before we knew the truth.
Before Friday was "Good."
Before Easter dawned
we were
children friendless,
men with no support,
women heartbroken.
Now we can sleep.
Now we can dream.

Miracle and Mystery!
The shadow land of Lent
has cascaded into brightness.
In the Lenten void
we could only long for Spring,
could only wait for the day,
wait for the ancient earnest rites,
the holy darkness of God's embrace,
the enveloping silence of our dreams,
the rushing waters of rebirth,
the oozing oil of gladness.
We could only wait for the Word,
wait for the mounting drama
and the stories.
Yes, those stories of death and resurrection.
Miracle and Mystery!
Now the stories and words explode
from the page.
They do more than sustain us.
They project us into a future
we thought we didn't have.
Fifty days of story and ritual.
Fifty days of singing and dancing.
Fifty days of joy the world doubted.
And those words
those stories
get under our skin
into our blood.
Miracle and Mystery!
Those rituals and words that
comfort and challenge us.
Those words that echo in our collective memory.

"You must not be afraid."
    An echo of Christmas angels.
"He is not here."
"Were not our hearts burning?"
"Do not touch me."

Then later:
"Take your finger and feel the wounds."
First, only words, and then!
Touch at last.
Ah, yes.
This new life is not some detached being
that hovers just out of reach.
Miracle and Mystery!
We approach and touch
to be transformed ourselves.
Miracle and Mystery!
The words and rituals last
not just for a night
but for fifty days
a lifetime
forever.
"Why stand there staring into the clouds?"
Miracle and Mystery!
Now our bodies
bear the message.
And I know I speak from a body
that could be lifeless
with sickness and sin, but...
Miracle and Mystery!
We use our bodies
to become one Body,
transformed and reborn.
We carry on.
We complete the Paschal picture.
Miracle and Mystery!
A second chance
with our own job to do,
our own story to tell,
our own song to sing.
Miracle and Mystery!

The world, of course,
has a foggy view
with its bad advice
and self-serving demands.
The world thinks heaven and earth
are separate.
It thinks the sacred and profane
cannot meet.
This attitude is schism!
A scandal!
A lie!
No,
Miracle and Mystery!
We are of a piece,
whole and integrated.
Irenaeus said:
"The Glory of God is human beings fully alive."
Like doubting Thomas
when we feel the wounds
we know he is not abstract,
not above our own gaping wounds
of sickness or sin,
not above our warring and wrangling,
not above our polluted rivers
our ravaged earth.
He waits only to be touched.
And in the touching
healing erupts on our landscape.
Miracle and Mystery!
Who would have guessed?
Who could predict?
Who will deny the day?
So here we come
unsuspecting sinners,
undeserving children of the
angry, hurting world.
Here we come
to plunge ourselves
headlong and heartfelt
into the
Miracle and Mystery of Easter.

THIRTY-FIVE YEARS OF ANGELS AND BREAD
1 Kings 19:4-8; Eph 4:30-5:2; John 6:41-51

Like most of us
Elijah might have preferred
to stay depressed,
lick his wounds,
feel sorry for himself.
His well-laid plans didn't materialize.
His projected little life didn't unfold
    —gentle and smooth—
in neat layers of love and satisfaction.
So why not lay down and die?
But God kept sending
Angels and Bread
Angels and Bread.
Get up and eat for the journey
he said,
the angel with the Bread.
And, in spite of himself
Elijah trudged all the way to Horeb
not willing, but obedient,
to face that mountain of God
with nothing more than an Angel
to fill his emptiness
and Bread to make him fly.
I've been there too
haven't you?
—Dragging my disappointments
and hurts
and any reason to delay
like a great steamer trunk
filled with too much ego
and not enough expansiveness,
avoiding the mountain,
looking for a broom tree
to settle under
and feel sorry for myself.

But then, surprise,
Angels and Bread
Angels and Bread
to keep me company
to fill my emptiness
to put the willow bend back
into my oakiness
and take the starch from the stiffness
of my neck.

When Jesus came along,
Power of the Father
Light of the World
and claimed to be nothing more than Bread,
he had to be thinking of Elijah
and you and me too.
And there was no dearth of angels.
At his Conception
    —Fear not Mary.
At his Birth
    —Gloria in Excelsis Deo.
At his Agony
    —Let this cup pass.
At his Resurrection
    —He is not here.
And so
like a great and shining arc of light
the Angels and Bread
span the centuries
leaping chasms
from Old Testament to New to Now
and keep us focused on the journey.
Once we are shaken awake
by that first Angel,
once we are enervated by that first Loaf
and come out from under the
smothering shade
of that prison broom tree,
planted in the arid desert
of our over-rated disappointment,
we discover that our lives
are punctuated
with Angels and Bread
Angels and Bread.

Angels in differing forms
no doubt,
where we least expect them.
Here an angel with healing hands
and warm embrace
to calm our fear
to carry us through.
There an angel with soothing voice
speaking to us
in the long and low-ceilinged
corridors of our isolation,
pulling us toward the light.
Their forms are so ordinary
we sometimes don't know they're Angels
until it's all over and we are moving again
to the mountain
not even missing the sloshing stifling sound
of our own lamentation.
And we smack ourselves in the head
and say: I think that was an angel!

Like the Angels
the Bread too comes in different shapes.
It nourishes us nonetheless.
Sometimes crusty
sometimes delicate
sometimes grainy
sometimes light.
Always satisfying the hunger
we didn't know we had.

When Jesus became our Bread
the possibilities became unlimited.
Anyone can be Bread now.
It's a hard pill to swallow
    —Some of "those" people who dare to be Bread!
    —Some of the characters Jesus allows himself to be!
When he gave his flesh as Bread
our own flesh too was redeemed
and everyone else's besides.

And life became precious.
When the little Jewish Boy
asked his Father
why everything living
and everyone he loves
must die,
the wise Father said:
"There is only one reason.
It is so life will be precious."
And so the Bread transforms even death
into something we don't recognize.
Life beyond life.
Life better than life.
His flesh for the life of the world.
Mary Magdalene found that out
when Jesus told her:
"Don't cling to the old me
there is a new life in store."
And the Angel told her:
"Wait, there's more!
Go tell the others.
(They've barred the door.)
But they have to come out.
There's Bread in store.
And now you even have Wine to pour."
It was once again
Angels and Bread
Angels and Bread
that sounded the call
we have all heard
again and again.

That is why, today
on this ordinary
but remarkable day,
a day made holy
by God's call and our gathering,
we join with that
proverbial cloud of witnesses
from Elijah and beyond,
to Jesus and today,
to tomorrow and forever.

We gather to open ourselves
to old certainties
and new possibilities.
And we will not be disappointed
because
now we know,
we gather to look
for nothing less than
Angels and Bread
Angels and Bread.

(This reflection was written as a homily for liturgy on August 10, 2003, to celebrate with my family and friends my 35th Year of Ordination.)

WILD RESURRECTION (Easter, 2004)

Do you know that Christ risen
can lightening out of the darkest sky
and be a morning sun to the
blackest night and the
hardest heart?
To Easter in us is no mean task.
We are thick-hearted
lapping, lazy
dreary, drowsy
cellar cold and proud
of our limited existence.
Arrogant,
we wear our stupidity
like a beleaguered badge of honor.
Who knew this Christ
could crack the stone with a laugh
and rise jubilant from the
damp, dark earth?
Who knew he would
take us with him
on a reeling, rousing journey of faith?
Drown us with rushing water.
Splash us with fragrant oil.
Clothe us with garments of love.
Who knew
there would be strong
heart-heavy bread to embolden us
and wondrous wine
rich as blood
to make us laugh
to give us a song?
Who knew he would invite us
into a dancing metaphor
for a life lived in leaps and bounds
over the dry parched earth
alive now with the greenest
freshest things?
Who knew?

Tip-toeing cautiously
toward the time-tied tomb
we discover eternity
breaking over us and flashing out
in fires of passion and love.
Who knew there would be angels
(again)
whisking us on raptured wings
into a new kind of knowing?
There was a chance
we would be stupid forever.
Then morning dawned
waterfalling over our lifeless brain
infusing even the dimwitted
with fresh thoughts
and mounting desire for life lived
always on the edge of love
holding out hope
for the brightest of days
and shimmering of nights...

Ahh!
And who knew there could be a calmness
in the face of fragility, brokenness and chaos?
Who knew?
Who knew that frenetic Alleluias
could quiet the most terrified soul
and bring the touch of Peace
from those wounded, risen hands?
In the excitement
spinning and rollicking wonder
there is the warmth to melt
the deep down dread
and icy-ness that
imprisons our world and
holds hearts hostage.
Who knew
wild resurrection could bring such a soothing embrace
to shivering souls?
Has anyone told the press?
Spare me the prophecies of gloom
and predictions of pandemonium.

Keep the bloody reports
and disgusting details.
Who knew?
You want news?
Here it is.
Christ is risen.
And even in the face of
frivolous facts
and depressing details
who knew
we could remain
unshaken in our resolve
firm in our faith
confident that the light of Resurrection
can shine in the bleakest man-made darkness?

Look up!
Orion, belted with brightness
hunts the midnight sky
stalking the honey-full moon.
Even he sees our little fire
        (glowing into a conflagration of Grace)
and he is distracted
delighted
deterred
from his pursuit
to look at what has happened
on this fractured redeemed planet.

And Jesus says: Amen, Alleluia!
And the Church says: Amen, Alleluia!

IN CALABRIA (2004)

<u>August 8</u>
The muse of words and magical sentences
sleeps in the remote corner of my mind
wrapped in shawls of silence.
Her timid face flashing
like an imprisoned moonbeam
waiting to be released
into the world of poetry and imagination
where children rule
and even the remotest possibility
is reality waiting to happen.

<u>August 16</u>
The eye of my mind
and indeed my whole body
remains filled with the image and feel
of the brazen Calabrian Sun
tenaciously climbing to the top
of the Aspromonte Mountains
arriving just in time to flail his savage locks
in a successful effort
to shake golden sunbeams
into every crevice and cliff
before he rolled head over heels
into the Tyrrhenian Sea
drenching himself out in a boiling inferno
of colors beyond any painter's palette.

THE GIFTS THAT MATTER (Christmas, 2004)

Winter Angel, Gabriel!
When you are finished
with your Christmas announcements
and clarion calls
Come!
Enfold me with your warm wings
for these are cold days
days of war and wrangling
and lying and losing
and deep down disappointment.
Yet we are not hopeless
and await the birth of the dazzling Sun
that promises to fly on bright beams
into the cold caverns we have constructed.

Gabriel!
Cover me with veils of deliverance.
Tidal wave me with oceans of acceptance.
I will be grateful for even
furrowed forgiveness on the field of life.
Sustain all of us
until he flashes forth on spectral stars.
And me, make me
by your embrace what you yourself are:
a message of God
a word spoken
boldly yet softly
into a hard world
that will not listen
to something as simple
as an angel's herald
or a child's cry
because computer chips
and satellites are the only
acceptable media
on our unraveling wavelength of wondering.
But the Word is not vindicated
by the listening
nor by claims of faithfulness.

Rather it stands on its own
for any who are willing to
open ears and hearts,
to breathe it in.

We say God is love.
So let me be a lover.
Someone else
someone somber
someone solemn
someone with no vision
can fret for the
dreary details of the dissolving day.
As for me
fill my eyes with clear sight.
Sight to see the transparent message
of the poor and outraged
who have been trampled upon
by the liars who dare to claim the name
Christian
while they manufacture their own gospel
and lay down rules no one has agreed upon.
Sight to see the shimmering spectacle
of a lustrous angel
who calmly brought a wondering virgin
to the door of birthing
nothing less than love itself.

To be lover
would be enough for me.
Enough for any
who wait for the luminous morning
of the Prince of Light.

Our old hideaways and havens evaporate.
Our old certainties and platitudes prove futile.
Our bodies betray us.
And age wearies us.
But Gabriel!
We will not be
helpless hopeless hindered.

Gabriel!
Bring on the Child.
Usher him on a flush of wings
into the cavity of a hollow world.
Let him epiphany in us.
We will be
renewed revitalized reminded
once again
of ancient promises that remain forever kept
by the very Heart of God
that throbs and sobs
for an obsessed and obdurate planet.

See what is good in us
what is worth saving
what needs a Child.
Even in our callousness and denial
you know that
we know the gifts that matter.
    The snow falling in lilting pillows
    and crunching under frosty feet.
    The warm wine drunk together in the glass of friendship
    by lives held together with commitment.
    The festive feasting at the groaning boards of family tables
    born solidly on the sturdy legs of the ones that nourish us.
    The unassuming heart that holds the sickbed hand tightly
    while it strains and prays to convey wellness.
    The kiss of lovers who long for the calligraphy
    of their own story carved on hearts of flesh.

O yes
in spite of our shallowness
we know the gifts that matter.
They lie unnumbered and unclaimed
strewn on the vapid sea
of our misguided navigation.
But we know the gifts that matter.
In the unfathomable depths
of the eternal heart
we know the gifts that matter.
So don't give up on us.

Messenger of Divine wisdom
announce to us once again
the Gift of God:
 the swaddling clothes and manger
 the shepherds and flocks
 the kings and camels
 the Peace on earth
 Mary, Joseph and
 the Child
 especially the Child.
Tell us again Gabriel
Winter angel.
Tell us again.

IF WE LIVE BY FAITH (Easter, 2005)

The winter birds are gone for sure.
The new bluebird houses are posted,
cleared and waiting.
The daffodils have cracked the frosty surface
and wait to bloom full,
sunshining the fallow ground with brilliance.
The mallards are waddling tentatively,
fuzzy down in their bills,
feathering their nests,
and waiting.
It seems everything waits.
It seems everything aches for Easter.
Everything looks to new life.

Me, I wait for the font to fill,
to fountain forth
free flowing
in a sparkle of sound and miniature waves.
I would wait for Gospel earthquakes
and scriptural angels
but Mary Magdalene has been there and done that
and so I must live by faith.
But I believe her and wait in my own way.

Me, I wait for the Word
to ring out from measured muteness,
to leap from the page,
to penetrate clogged ears
and hardened hearts.
I have been told it has a special power,
a glorious grace
when it dances from faithful lips.
I believe that.

Me, I wait for the fire to flash out
in burning bright opalescence.
Unlike that first Easter morning
no strange beings lightening into my life,
no mesmerizing messenger in snowy white
helps me measure my time.
Did I mention we live by faith.
And it is enough.

Me, I wait for the oil to fragrance its way
into the nostrils of my consciousness
and allay my fear of the smell of death.
I know something Mary and the women didn't.
He is not in the tomb.
But, alas, the Risen Christ is harder to find
than an entombed body.
Entombed bodies always stay put.
But a Risen Lord?
In unlikely places?
In impossible people?
In sickness and sadness?
Much harder to uncover
than an obedient dead body.
Indeed, we live by faith.
I think I told you that.

Me, I wait at the Table.
A Table without boundaries
and a banquet without seating charts.
A Table of Plenty,
groaning under the weight of the centuries
but weightlessly dancing its way into my range of vision.
A Table where Jesus
greets us on the way
washes our feet
prepares a place
and makes incredible promises
that the world will not believe.
But we live by faith...
by now, we've agreed on that.

For us then,
the incredible becomes commonplace
the unlikely is expected
and there are no impossible dreams.
No one is ever turned away
when the Lord sets the Table...
Is the Host...and the Guest...
Is the Hunger...and the Food...
Is the Hope...and the Fulfillment.
And it is by faith we find a place
at this Table.
No one doubts it now.

All of us live by faith.
We wouldn't be here otherwise.
And in that faith
we just do what we always do.
Even on this
Great Feast of Easter
we do what we always do.
We gather around
Water
Word
Fire
and Table.

Sustained by these, we wait for Jesus
to meet us on the way,
to meet us in the Water,
to meet us in the Word,
to meet us in the Fire,
to meet us at the Table,
to meet us in the face of the poor,
to meet us...in the mirror.
If we live by faith
we will see him,
maybe not as envisioned in our pre-conceptions,
but exactly as He is.

WILL YOU BE A WONDER (Christmas, 2005)

Sweet Honey in the Rock taught me a song*:
THERE IS A BALM IN GILEAD
THAT MAKES THE WOUNDED WHOLE.
THERE IS A BALM IN GILEAD
THAT CURES THE SIN-SICK SOUL.

> Will you be a wonder?
> Will you be a healing balm for hurting hearts?

I have known Advents
that were like
frenzied search parties
picking through the aching streets
in search of a respite from pain
canvassing the tormented hills
hoping for relief.

Such an Advent
is not the prescribed patient waiting
or hopeful expectation
but more the frantic search
for something
—anything—
to give life.

> Will you be a wonder?
> Will you be a healing balm for hurting hearts?

Sometimes we make our own racket
of course
to allay our fears
to fulfill our own prophecies of doom.
How can one hear the voice
of an announcing angel
above the din
of fear or worry
of self-pity and doubt
of war cries and lies?
Our lives do not roll gently
from the mythic hills
into homes of embering hearths and home cooked meals.

We do not live in a peaceful country
where show-stopping shepherds
lull about on a starry desert retreat
waiting for an angel trumpet.
It is only that way
in the Bethlehem of our nostalgia.

    Will you be a wonder?
    Will you be a balm for hurting hearts?

Today and here as then in Bethlehem
war-ravaging kings
butcher Rachel's children
kill our young men and women
and vilify what they do not comprehend.
Christ must go underground
with his message of peace and goodwill
for those who seek out the secret places
and listen with their hearts
rather than their pocketbooks
or political aspirations
or fears.
Oh, but there are signs
for the watchful eye.
There are promises
for the hopeful heart.

    Will you be a wonder?
    Will you be a balm for hurting hearts?

The moon at its fullest
creeps silently over the far hill
and rolls gently down
behind the tall pines
splintering the inky black night
with shards of white light.
At the cabin window
I wait and watch
like a child
impatient and unfocused
watch for a leaping stag
wait for a light
to penetrate wintry wills.

And when I am finally quieted
the smooth and comforting
darkness velvets over our common soul
nestling warmly in the inmost reaches
of the most tortured hearts
    silencing screams
    quenching thirst
    satisfying even a raging hunger
for just one fragile and everlasting night.

    Will you be a wonder?
    Will you be a balm for hurting hearts?

Augustine said that
people travel to wonder
at the heights of the mountain tops
at the huge waves of the sea
at the long courses of the rivers
at the vast compass of the ocean
at the circular motion of the stars
—and they pass by themselves without wondering.

    Will you be a wonder?
    Will you be a balm for hurting hearts?

Tonight take time
to wonder at yourself
for you are indeed a source of wonder.
Take a moment to feel the soothing balm
gently flowing from your own hands.
Because of one holy night
one holy child
one breathless moment
you are a wonder.
Because of one holy night
the healing balm no longer languishes in Gilead
but surges inside you.

    Will you be a wonder?
    Will you be a healing balm for hurting hearts?

The wonder that you are
is called incarnation.
The balm that you become
is a soothing ointment called grace.

It is true that
because of our egos and posturing
and attempts to play power
we have forgotten the wonder within
buried it
ashamed of our own tenderness.
We have allowed the balm to dry
and become brittle within us
insecure with our own strength.
But the wonder within
is the power of God
breathed into the spirit
that soars in each one of us.
The balm is a healing river
that can surge again.
You are each of you a wonder
each of you a healing balm.
There are days of doubt
but yes
I am a wonder.
I am balm.
It is not about perfection or accomplishment
or anything measurable by human standards.
It is of God.
It is of this holy and beautiful night
that will not be highjacked
by political correctness
or meaningless chatter.
The realization that you are a wonder
that you are a healing balm
that a child has been born in you
—that realization alone
will propel you into horizons
beyond the limitations
of your own mind.
A muddled world may not know
but the expansive closet of your imagination
is big enough for angels to fly around
and echo through the unchartered wisdom courses
of the landscape lingering there
anticipating discovery.

You too can be
one of those wonder-filled people
who when you take time to know them
are like a great mounting wave
that washes over you and
more than covers you on the outside
but fills you up inside too
so that just the encounter
is a knowing of something
greater than themselves.
Who is not a wonder
on this DAY of deep grace?
Even angels would be nothing
without a message to herald
into the midnight stars
and the canvassing night sky.
Who would decline being a balm
for a fractured world?
Even nomadic magi
from mysterious latitudes
carry gold, incense and myrrh
to the most humble places.

      Will you be a wonder?
      Will you be a healing balm for hurting hearts?

Angels report that you can do it.
Shepherds look into the sky of your heart and spread the word.
Magi in their noble meanderings predict your gifts.
And a Child says you will.

(*"There is a Balm in Gilead," a traditional African American spiritual)

LET THE MYSTERY BE (Easter, 2006)

Let the Mystery Be!
Here we come,
cautiously from the silence,
tenuously from the darkness,
our hearts set on resurrection
and our eyes waiting for sunshine.
But we can Let the Mystery Be!
Hope is a strange thing indeed.
It propels us into the future
while at the same time,
it makes the impoverished present moment palatable.
But Hope expects fulfillment.
We have had enough of
silence and darkness.
Purpled for 40 Days
we need some yellow and orange
splashed onto our dark lifescape.
Still, we can Let the Mystery Be!
So, indeed, here we come
into this Easter Night,
this Night of Nights,
this Queen of all Feasts.
Tonight we remember
that though we wander through time
we remain anchored in eternity.
Having weathered the Lenten season
we know that the windmill of faith
spins boldly even on the hill of
an unbelieving landscape.
It generates the power to make the incredible
more than believable.
It lights up cities of souls sheared
of life.
It bathes even the most repressive canvas
of depression and destitution
with an abundance of color
and frames it with a future
no one thought possible.
Indeed, Let the Mystery Be!

How could we know?
The disciples doubted.
The women searched among the dead.
The tomb became
like a Nautilus split open,
halved and chambered
with neatly arranged windows on the world.
Life tiptoeing on the rim of chaos
has now become Life unleashed
on a surprised world.
Ah, Let the Mystery Be!
We have kissed the Cross
but we have no illusions about
its savage power and
its incredible lightness.
Is it death or life?
It is indeed deep murky Mystery!
Let the Mystery Be!
Roaring fires,
Flickering candles,
Stories whispered and shouted,
Flowing Water,
Oil erupting from the crystal decanter,
Bread and Wine.
You want to understand this?
Let it be Mystery. Let the Mystery be.
Easter is not an exercise of the mind.
It is the fierce business
of the heart held firmly in place
by the hand of God.
Bear your splinter of the Cross
and walk boldly into tomorrow
but Let the Mystery Be!
Grasp your fragile bit of flame
and light up the dark canyon in someone's heart
and Let the Mystery Be!
Listen to the story told again and again,
speak it even to a deaf ear
and Let the Mystery Be!
Navigate these Waters.
Carry them in buckets to parched lives
but Let the Mystery Be!

Inhale the fragrance of the Holy Oils
and stir a balm for wounded souls
but Let the Mystery Be!
Consume the Bread and Wine
and in the strength of this holy food
become the Mystery
you cannot understand.
Live the Mystery
you cannot explain.
Let the Mystery be! Let the Mystery be!
Let yourself be the Mystery.

FEAST OF GREAT ABUNDANCE (Christmas, 1980/2006)

(Over a quarter of a century ago, before my St. Luke days, I wrote some words. At the urging of a few people, I wish to share those words again.)

All Christmases
are like bells
ringing down my memory
shaking down like snow,
settling,
resting in hearts' pockets
and minds' crevices.

The bells ring
and I am a child
sharing noisy Christmas Eves
with the special ones
who extended my family,
tender aunts and grouchy uncles
who loved me nonetheless
and helped trade
quite early
my Santa Claus for a Christ Child
who always slept
under the tree
instead of in the bedroom
with us...
And even then I wondered why,
remembering
as I drifted off,
not so much the wrapped and foiled
packages
but more
the pomegranates, nuts, oranges
and fruit cake
that weighed down the groaning board
that tabled and fellowshipped us
more than Christians realize.

And in another ring
of the memory bells
I am a youth
like some and unlike others
still looking through the angel hair
like a child,
waiting for shepherds to speak
and wanting Magi
to dismount their camels and
epiphany in me
so I could know their wisdom
and not search for my own answers
but all along being sure,
as sure as the bells,
that no one else's answers
would be good enough for me
whose life was littered with
question mark snowflakes
drifting
and blowing the tinsel away
leaving me face to face,
not with a plaster Christ child
but with the Jesus of Faith
whose gaze shoots through
the haze, the maze
and pierces my soul
like the icicles
that snap from the spouting
and go screaming into the snow.

The tongues in the bells
strike again
and I am at the unspeakable time of life
when faith became a reality
and ideas took shape
becoming convictions
that echoed the staggering voices
of the shaggy haired prophets
who thundered down the centuries
stopping at my door
with their justice and Jesse roots:
—Micah walking humbly with his God
—Hosea searching the prostituted streets for his people

—Amos demanding food for the hungry
—Ezekiel dancing with dry bones
—Jeremiah protesting he is too young (Alas, not so for me anymore)
—Isaiah shouting virgins and peaceable kingdoms into being
—John deluging the earth in madman fashion.
All of them
plodding, streaming
whispering, screaming
out of the past
frustrating our attempts
to turn Christmas
into a mere holiday
wassailed into a bowl or
postage stamped into a corner
of our year.

Now the bells ring up another memory.
Minister of the Word
proclaimed
incarnate.
And how did I get here?
The scent of pine
needles into my nostrils
and hangs...
like the heavily snowed boughs
that creak and groan
under the weight of responsibility.
Who will bake the bread?
Who will crush the grapes?
The crisp night and sharp stars
crack out an answer
as some brave travelers
bundle up the snapping wind
and allow a child
to Eucharist in them.
The houses in (my southern) hills
sparkle with
poverty put to rest
if only for tonight
when we are all rich
having shared the unspeakable.

And tonight...
Memories in the making
and still the bells ringing
now punctuated and counterpointed
with pipes and drums
and flutes and strings.
A tradition alive and present.
Let the Word go out,
unfurled like a flag
blowing like a banner.
The Word
flashing across our lives
like a falling star
whipping like driven snow
salted from the shaker sky.
Let the Word go out.

>   And let the Bread be broken
>   for those who have died
>   or lived
>   for no reason.
>   Let the Bread be broken
>   for a Child's sake,
>   let the Bread be broken.

>   And the Wine.
>   Let the Wine run free
>   coursing through our lives
>   swirling, bubbling
>   water-falling over our cliffed madness,
>   flooding our parched personalities,
>   decanted and poured
>   into our cupped existence.
>   Let the wine run free.

It's Christmas!
Proclaim the Word
Break the Bread
Pour the Wine
Ring the Bells
so that one more Christmas
can be memoried and treasured,
cached (cased) into the arsenal of Peace.

(Additional reflection, 2006: this Christmas, 26 years later, life has given me something to add.)

And now
the Bells continue to ring
sometimes with a more urgent clap,
sometime with an excited, pulsating peel
and more recently, with a measured strike,
bordering on a toll.
     (And we all know for whom the bell tolls.)
But it is not cause for tears.
If this Advent has been a journey
from Darkness to Light
it is only a paradigm for life itself.

The world will always need someone
to charge fearlessly
into the darkness of poverty and hunger,
into the darkness of sickness and death.
And each foray
into that unknown and threatening place
shines a light so penetrating
that ordinary folks
feel empowered
to negotiate the blackest landscape
for themselves
and for brothers and sisters
they didn't know they had.

Have you ever hidden
in the dark spaces of your own life
wondering if anyone
will ever find you
or even try?
I have.
Making sense of the darkness
can only happen
when one lives
on the edge of each minute
looking for the light
looking for love.

The finding is not as important as the looking
for the looking itself opens up vistas
of unfathomable abundance.

Tonight is the Feast of Great Abundance.
How could a loving God have given us more?
Tonight is the Feast of Great Abundance.
Ring the Bells. Ring in the Light.
Ring the Bells.
Ring the Bells.

BURNING BUSHES & FIG TREES (Lent, 2007)

I've never seen a burning bush
and God knows I've looked.
Especially on those crackling Fall days
as I head out alone,
walking
down the hills and along the towpath,
when the woods seem to be already in flame.
It always seems a perfect day for a burning bush.
And I always think it might happen.
Once or twice I've seen
      from the corner of my eye
      what I thought was a flash
and even heard a crackling,
as of fire.
But turning quickly I discover
it is only a humble autumn olive
clinging tenaciously to the hillside shale,
while at the same time
dropping some of its autumn leaves
in a cascade of winter preparation.
Then I am reminded,
once again,
that even in his sinfulness,
Moses was the one on fire,
smoldering with the Word,
a blazing man of prayer,
ardent with the presence of God.
I knew that!
The fire must come from within
to consume my sinfulness
and make space,
not for burning shrubbery
but for a God on fire with love for me.

Now fig trees are another story,
not as mysterious as burning bushes.
I know about fig trees.
The rich green leaves
with nothing to pick.
The appearance of health
on fruitless branches.

213

The disappointment.
I've seen that.
But then
I've also seen
the care, the tending, the time,
the acrid manure, a pungent penance no doubt.
I've waited the one more season.
Often it takes no more
to yield the rich purple fruit.
The brilliant color
bursting into sweetness,
picked from the tree,
still holding the September sun in its pulp.
This mythical fruit
coupled with a glass of wine
and a slice of cheese far outstrips
a seven course dinner.
It is surprising sometimes
the kind of meal that nourishes us!
Yes, I know about fig trees.
And so I know about redemption.
The chance to find fruitfulness
even in my barrenness.
The blessing of Sacred Time
that sets us free of our
self-imposed bondage,
our leafy cover,
our fruitless branches
and even our self-indulgent prayer.
The blessing of Sacred Time
that calls us to something more
than we thought possible.
Burning bushes and fig trees.
Setting fires and cultivating fruit.
Now is the Sacred Time.

AN AFTER-EASTER DIARY (2007)

We gather in darkness
outside the church doors in our courtyard,
a large cauldron boasts a raging fire.
Even in the hushed atmosphere
there is an audible murmur of excitement
and tangible anticipation
as people encircle the flames.
The chill in the air is cut
not only by fire
but by the proximity of a people
burning with hope.
The priest blesses the New Fire.
He blesses the Paschal Candle too.
We hold our common breath
as he bends close to the flames
to light a taper
that will ignite our Christ Light.
And there it is!
A flicker at first,
then set ablaze,
a single flame
yet bright enough to light up hearts
in the darkness of sin.
What is this Candle?
Why is it so special?
Is it the pillar of fire
that lead the Israelites to safety?
Is it the flame of the Spirit?
Is it the very presence of the Christ among us?
Yes, yes and yes.
It is all these and more.
It is the "more" that calls us
into the church building
to become the Church
that cannot be contained by walls.

The deacon holds the candle aloft and walks.
We follow.
LUMEN CHRISTI!
The candidates and elect are first.
Then the ministers of the altar.

Then the rest of us,
the young and old,
the infirm and the strong,
hearts bursting with anticipation.
The flagging ones too...
the ones who are tentative...
the ones who are yearning...
the ones who don't even know why they are here.
We all follow through the church doors.
LUMEN CHRISTI.
Our little lights are ignited.
The pews are filling now.
Will there be enough room?
Certainly, room for all.
All faces are awash with warm light.
LUMEN CHRISTI.

Now our space is infused with light.
The darkness is overcome.
Evaporated before our very eyes.
We take our places.
"Is everybody here?
Does everybody have a place to bide?
Is everybody safe and warm inside?"
There is a moment of steeling.
Then...
the ancient text of the Easter Proclamation
—the Exultet—is sung.
The melody is wrapped in candle light
and born on the wings of hope.
It fills our space with beautiful sound.
The words are a treasure
of the Christology
of the desert Fathers
and Mothers of the Church.
Using the imagery of Christ as light,
it touches on themes of
Exodus and Sacrifice
Atonement and Liberation
Covenant and New Life.
It is sung lovingly and with passion.
Still holding our candles aloft
we savor the poetry and the theology.

The refrain rings in our ears
resonates in our hearts.
It is at once triumphant exaltation
and wondering contemplation.
This is the night!
This is the night!
"This is the night when Christians everywhere, washed clean of sin,
and freed from all defilement, are restored to grace and grow
together in holiness."
Again, what is this flame
that we can sing to it,
even dance around it?
It is the renewed fire of faith in our own lives.

Now we sit.
We are anxious to hear the long story,
our history of salvation.
We don't leave anything out.
We want to hear it all.
We can never hear enough of this,
the reprise of our transformation
and God's action in our lives.
Genesis and Exodus
Isaiah and Baruch
Ezekiel and Paul.
We savor every word.
We know the story well.
We can tell it in our own words.
This story is in our bones
and in our brains
in our hearts and in the communal memory.

Then a great acclamation!
The Gospel Book is carried through the assembly.
With singing and dancing
tambourines and streamers
pipes and drums
strings and reeds
and the organ bearing it all on bright wings.
The children process,
no it is more like running!
They are following the Gospel Book
singing and smiling.

In them our youth is rekindled,
no, unbridled.
The deacon proclaims the Gospel story
in the words of the great Evangelist.
And we do not merely HEAR the story.
No, it happens again in our midst.
Now we know why we are here:
TO PROCLAIM THE DYING AND RISING OF CHRIST THE LORD.

The homily helps us
to reflect on the Word
to lift the word from the page
and plant it deep within our hearts.
We hear the Good News.
We become the Good News.

Now is the moment we have all been waiting for.
The time when the Elect
are received into the Church.
Through Baptism, Confirmation and Holy Eucharist
they will be one with us.
We have watched them
all through the Lenten season.
Now they walk forward and stand before us.
As they move
we begin to sing the Litany of the Saints,
not a tiresome chant
but an enthusiastic calling
upon the host of heaven
to be with us in this solemn moment
of personal commitment
and communal celebration.
And we light our candles again
so they can find us.
Holy Mary Mother of God
St. Joseph
St. Andrew
St. Paul
St. Luke
St. Anthony
St. Brigid.
No one is left out.

All are summoned
from the heavenly hall
to our humble gathering place.
And come they do.
We can feel them next to us,
all around us,
over our heads and in our hearts.
Not one of them would miss
this great event of Church revival.
Nor would we.
Now the water is blessed.
The waters of creation...
the waters of the great flood...
the waters of the Jordan...
the waters of Baptism.
How does God do all that,
cram all those images
into one humble baptismal pool?
Renunciation of sin.
Profession of faith.
A solemn moment.
Now before we know it,
those being baptized step into the water.
Maybe if they really knew
the depth of what was involved
they might run from that pool.
But no,
it is a plunge of faith.
The priest stands in the font
ready to greet them.
They stand up
glowing, breathless, soaked, smiling, crying
and are lead out by assistants
to change into dry clothing.
We begin singing:
"I saw water...Alleluia."
And they return
to be enveloped in our song and in our prayer.
"You have put on Christ," we sing.
Then all are confirmed.
Veni Sancte Spiritus. Veni Sancte Spiritus.
And the Spirit comes indeed.

The scent of the Holy Chrism
assures us of that
as it wafts over the whole assembly.
This night has a fragrance all its own.

Without time to catch our breath
the time flies by,
we move into Eucharist.
The altar is prepared
and the gifts are presented.
"The Lord be with you...
Lift up your hearts..."
We have indeed lifted them up.
Then the familiar words of the Eucharistic Prayer
fill our banquet hall.
And it begins to dawn on us
that it is more than the Bread and Wine
that are being changed
into the Body and Blood of Christ.
You can feel the transformation.
You can hear more than ever
that we are one voice,
one heart,
one Body.

The first communicants make their way to the altar,
some tentative,
some leaning hopefully into the Mystery,
all hungry for the Bread of Life
and the Cup of Salvation.
And we sing.
We always sing.
Pan de Vida...
Taste and See...
In Christ There Is a Table Set for All.
We sing as we make our way
in solemn yet joy-filled procession
to the Altar of Sacrifice, the Table of Plenty.
In receiving this One Bread and One Cup
we become One Body.
And we remember the words of St. Augustine:
"Say Amen to your own mystery.
Eat what you are...become what you eat."
And so we do.

Now, back in our places again,
there is a brief pang of disappointment.
It is almost over.
All those months the catechumens prepared,
all those choir practices,
all the preparation,
all the anticipation...
We want to live in the moment forever.
Have we just had a foretaste
of the Banquet Feast of Heaven?
This Glorious Easter Vigil,
this queen of feasts,
this night of nights!
The priest gathers all our prayers into one,
a simple understated prayer,
and then we are sent forth,
sent to carry this Mystery to a hungry world.
And the singing again.
Alleluia. Alleluia.
Jesus Christ Is Risen Today.
Over My Head I Hear Singing in the Air.
Alleluia. Alleluia. Alleluia.

IN A MOMENT OF SILENCE (For a friend, 2007)

Often the geometry of my life
over which I have no control
slices at harsh angles
against my hopes of what could be.
My thoughts sluice
like strong water birds
through the murky estuary
of a world on the edge of drowning.
Then of a sudden
these thoughts flutter and hang
like fickle finches and hummingbirds
at thistle and trumpet vine
looking for a nectar that will
sustain the future.

Life is seldom calm.
It can be a volcanic eruption
that soots and ashes itself
over the bucolic valleys
of the neatly furrowed fields
in our controlled existence.

Or at best
Life is a light breeze
wafting unaware
high above thrashing waters
and erupting waves.

But it is always
Faith that keeps us from suffocating
Hope that keeps us from drowning
Love that keeps us suspended in mid-air.

And so we hide,
each of us
in the spaces of our own life
wondering if anyone
will ever find us
or even try?

Yet, making sense of life
can only happen
when one lives
on the edge of each minute
looking for love.
The finding
is not as important
as the looking.
For the looking
opens up vistas
of unfathomable abundance.

A LONE FIGURE (Lake Erie, 2007)

It was one of those spectacular mornings,
the water undulating,
the lake breeze strong and cool,
the sun brilliant and mottled into
abstract patterns through the tree line
along the beach's edge.

I watched, from a distance,
a lone figure on the sand,
quite content, it seemed,
to be alone
watching the lake
like some folks watch a TV screen,
mesmerized by the motion
or maybe just lost in his own thoughts.
I imagine him
working through some difficult problem
waiting for the waters
and his emotions
to calm and smooth out.
Yet content to wrestle with
his own angel and wait to see
what will be whispered into his ear
—a minor revelation
or a major epiphany.
It doesn't matter.

That unknown figure became a gift,
an icon for the life of faith,
an icon for any who would dare
to commit to service and prayer
in an often fickle world
and in a Church
with all its humanity,
fraught with crisis,
with all its divinity,
a sign and an instrument
of the Kingdom of God.

From A NIAGARA OF GRACE (Easter, 2008)

The Jesus of our faith
died, rose and became a people.
So says the theologian Aidan Kavanagh.
Jesus is us!
That is harder to believe in
than Resurrection,
don't you think?
Besides,
it is too much responsibility
to be Christ for others.
But the early Christians
never believed that the Easter Mystery
was some divine cardiopulmonary resuscitation.
Oh no, they knew that Christian Faith
is the experience of the Empowering Presence
of Jesus the Lord.
Maybe that is why the Scriptures
never describe the event
        the phenomenon
of Jesus rising from the tomb.
Oh yes,
we read of earthquakes and angels.
But no eyewitness account of
what happened to Jesus.
Only the aftermath,
the appearances,
the discovery.
Yes, the presence!
He becomes a friend in the garden.
Mary Magdalene wanted Jesus back,
but as she knew and remembered him.
She wanted yesterday.
She didn't get that.
Then she wanted him in a grave
she could visit and tend.
She didn't get that.
She got a friend in the Garden.
A Friend she didn't recognize.
A Friend who knew her name...
        and called her...
        called her to be the apostle to the apostles.

And what about the disciples on the road?
They wanted to erase the past,
lament the events of yesterday,
hunker down and lick their wounds.
They wanted their old Jesus back.
But they didn't get that.
They got a Companion at Table,
a Companion they didn't recognize,
a new Presence.

And what about us?
We can't have Jesus on our own terms either.
We can't have him as a warm memory
or a dearly departed whose grave
we can visit.
Jesus is alive
and ahead of us
calling us forward.
We want to stand still and be sure
rather than move forward into the unknown...
forward on a new path whose turnings
we can't anticipate.

Judas and Peter and Pilate
will wake up to find
it was not a bad dream.
They have to decide
what to do with their sin.
And so do we.
Because Jesus did not rise
to prove us right.
He rose to prove us forgiven.
Indeed, we must decide what to do
with all our sin
and all God's forgiveness.

And make no mistake about it,
there is an abiding connection
between the Jesus of Nazareth
and the Jesus of Resurrection.
Jesus of Nazareth was not just a thinker
with ideas,
he was a rebel with a cause
—a peasant with an attitude.

But there are not two Jesuses
only one...alive in us.
So we must take on the cause.
We must acquire the attitude.
Don't ask what happened to Jesus.
Ask what is happening to you.
Easter is never an empty tomb.
It is a full heart...
full and overflowing
with forgiveness, healing and New Life.

I CHOOSE TO LIVE (Lake Erie, 2008)

In the park
each blade of grass
shouts and shimmers
reflecting the sun
basking in the breeze
whispering to one another
"Let's go for a swim."
But alas
they are each one of them
earthbound like me.
It is strange
that such a beautiful
and vibrant morning
should elicit
thoughts of death.
Not just thoughts
reflections really.
I wonder if there will ever be
a time when
I will embrace death.
Is there an age
or a moment
when one does not pray
to get well
to have health
to have "one more day"
I wonder?
This morning I am peaceful
and content.
I revel in my aloneness.
Yet I feel connected to everyone and everything.
Is this a moment
when I could die
unembarrassed and unafraid?
When I could embrace
my physical limits?
The sickness
the failing body
the pain
the anxiety?

Is this a time
when youthful enthusiasm
and aging awareness
could come together and shout
without hesitation or fear:
"I am ready?"
And yet
I feel so alive.
No pain.
No anxiety.
No worry.
No fear.
And so it is another day
I choose to live
and celebrate
those glittering blades
in the park
that whispering breeze
off the lake
and most of all
that blinding sun
that binding sun
singing and dancing
over the waters
shouting
Here I am!
Here I am!

REMEMBERING JOE: "Bigger Life"

Joe had a passion for making everything come to *bigger life*. Dinner for three grew to a party with eight, or ten, or twenty...a pound of pasta became a gourmet dish, with a new twist to an old recipe. He liked gatherings to have meaning and *bigger life*. Breakfast with staff prompted ideas and plans...lunch preceded most meetings and became its own event...supper was a good time to share stories. Whatever he was thinking, saying, doing, always escalated into something much bigger. If he was alone, he put it on paper to be shared later, in the form of poetry, prayer, or agenda.

His gardens were a celebration of *bigger life*. Joe planted and plucked shrubs, bushes, vines, flowers, and seeds...everywhere...inside and outside the rectory, the cabin, and along country roads. In summer, he bordered paths with purple blooming fennel and gave it life beyond the yard. You could find it displayed in a vase; hanging upside down drying at the kitchen window; crushed in an herb container; and framed under glass hanging as art.

Most of all, Joe loved bringing people together at Liturgy, to open God's Word and give thanks in Eucharist. Celebrating Mass refreshed his spirit and renewed his hope. He was always looking for ways to share that gift. He wanted time at Mass to have meaning for us, for the mission to become our daily routine...and for a *bigger life*. Joe lived Eucharist and continued that celebration at the dining table...his art bench...his desk...

Joe knew that hope is a gift from within and all around, a gift from God. He lived out that hope in his darkest days. It helped him to endure sadness throughout his ministry and years of trials with his own health. He shared with us his many thoughts and prayers about living and dying—and living a *bigger eternal life*—that we might witness to others. Thank you, Joe, for drawing us closer to God by your powerful message of celebration and hope in the midst of life's blessings and challenges.

—Donna Mertes

CHAPTER SEVEN
ST. LUKE IV (2009-2015)

COMPASSION AND KINDNESS (Easter, 2009)

What were they thinking?
Those women trundling off to the tomb?
It had probably taken six soldiers
to lever that boulder into place.
And here they come
armed with spices and perfume
to do their thing.
What were they thinking?
But as always
compassion and kindness
trump common sense.
I need to remember that.
Compassion and kindness
trump common sense.
Maybe with that in mind
we can hear the Easter call
to roll away the rocks
that seal our hopes and dreams
in tombs of despair and cynicism.

In his resurrection
Christ unleashes powers
that common sense can never muster.
Compassion and kindness
justice peace and reconciliation
transform our world
in a way common sense never could.

Do you want to move the boulder of discouragement?
Do you need to pry open the tomb of fear?
What boulder is blocking change for you?
What stone is weighing you down?
Go ahead, make a list.
    —A country perpetually immersed in wars
    of empire and greed.
    —An economy that imprisons ordinary people
    and breaks the backs of the poor.
    —A society where life is cast aside
    for expediency or false security.
    —A church where a pharisaical adherence to the past
    denies people ministry and hope.
    —A family where old grudges
    block forgiveness and reconciliation.
    —A religion that places political agendas
    before faith and tradition.
Make your list.
And it is only the beginning.
The losses, the hurts,
the betrayals, the sickness,
the dying.
They are endless.
But consider this:
    As we peer into the empty tomb
    with Mary Magdalene and the women,
    with Peter and John,
    we can be as confused as they were.
    We can be as scared as they were.
    When they set out that morning
    there was no such thing as Easter.
    Not as a word.
    Not as a concept.
    Certainly not as a hope held out
    to people like you and me.
    And it doesn't make common sense.
Who were the first ones to discover Easter?
Mary Magdalene and the women
who stayed at the Cross to the end
and who didn't have enough sense
to be prepared.
They discovered Easter first.

And then Peter,
the one who denied him,
the one who never got it.
He discovered Easter next.
And then the other disciple,
the one Jesus loved,
John no doubt.
He is at the tomb too.
Common sense would expect
historians, writers, newscasters,
social commentators and heads of state.
But no!
The resurrection is revealed
in particular ways to particular people
according to each one's particular relationship
with Jesus.
Not according to their relationship
with the world.
Jesus does not love
some abstract humanity,
does not reveal his resurrection
in abstract generalities.
No, Jesus loves persons.
Jesus reveals his resurrection to personal community.

So how does Jesus
reveal his resurrection to you?
Remember,
common sense doesn't work.
So how does he do it?
First he takes hope
that the stone says we dare not trust.
Then he takes joy
that the boulder declares will be betrayed.
Next he takes dreams
that the rock tells us to keep hidden.
He unwraps all these things
from burial bands and calls it Easter.
That's how he does it.

And how do we do it?
How do we claim Easter?
How do we take it in?
First of all,
we cast common sense aside.
We do foolish things
that the world deems silly.
We gather in Holy Darkness
    and we are not afraid.
We actually think Christ will be our Light!
We ignite a raging fire
    to warm the Lenten chill.
We become people burning with hope.
We light a Candle
    so the Saints can find us.
Remember, we said it doesn't make sense.
We sing songs of liberation and life
    to give the world hope.
We don't care what the practical say.
We fill our space with music and dance
    for the deafness and infirmity in all of us.
We tell those ancient stories
    incredible to the untrained ear.
We think it is our story!
We proclaim the Gospel
    with unbounded faith and youthful enthusiasm.
We smile at the child in each of us.
We sing the saints and angels into our humble church.
We profess a faith that challenges the mighty.
No common sense here.
We plunge people into pools of water
    teeming with symbolism, new birth and life forever.
We oil them with gladness
    and the fragrance fills our space.
We clothe them with white garments
    and we all are somehow innocent again.
We fire them with love
    and no one is excluded.
We fill them with Bread from heaven
    and all partake of the one loaf.

And here common sense is truly challenged.
Take and eat.
Take and drink.
    Does he mean me?
This is my body.
This is my blood.
    It doesn't make sense.
Who can believe it?
Who can understand it?
Who can make sense of it?
Remember?
We set common sense aside.
Remember?
We are people of mystery and symbol.
Remember?
We become what we eat and drink.
Who needs common sense?
We have common faith.
And it will bear us up
on Resurrection wings
to a Glory no stone can hold back.

FOR AUNT MARGARET (June 22, 2009)

When those women
were amazed by an angel
they didn't know
at first
they were part of something
    —something bigger than their own sorrow
    —something more important than the task at hand
    —something greater than life itself.
They probably didn't know
that if life is indeed a journey
then this thing called death
is a destination...
a destination into the very heart of Christ.
And they may not have known
but they did discover
that on this journey
there is more than
one angel hiding
in the events and people
in the turns and challenges
of our lives.
The empty tomb
the Resurrection of Jesus
the Christ Event
changes all the rules
shifts all the experiences
moves all the pieces
fulfills all the promises.
Now there are angels in every joy
divine messengers in every hurt
winged wonders around every corner.
Now everything is about life
even, and most especially, death itself.
We struggle with
the hollowness in our chest
the dashed plans littering our minds
the shades and shadows of the human heart
which too often keep us from seeing
the openness and light of Divine Love.

When Anthony died
I remember
Aunt Margaret lamented that
she could not make him warm again
    —a mother's concern, no doubt.
It took time for her to know
that angels had whisked him away
on bright wings
into a place of brilliant light
and thin, thin air.
She was sad for a long time.
But then,
one morning, by sheer will,
she chose to move from
the darkness of despair
into the light of an ordinary morning
with a sky full of shimmering wings
and bright wonder.
In that movement
she found angels
darting about
pulling her heart
into a new place.

When Aunt Margaret died
someone asked how
she could be warm one minute
and so cold the next.
Ah, but angels move quickly
and if you are blessed
you can feel
the coolness and refreshment
of the embracing waters of eternal Baptism
that cascade over every sadness
and wash every tremor away.

When Jesus died
there were some who ran off.
But that's not important.
Even they figured it out eventually.

More important is knowing
there were those who remained
   —who kept watch
   —who made vigil
   —who counted every anguished breath
   —who took him into their arms
   —who held him close.
We were blessed to do that for Margaret.
Sisters and children
grandchildren and family
friends and neighbors
all hiding unknown angels
   —in arms full of food
   —in words and in silence
   —in distraught faces
   —in questioning eyes
   —in failing bodies
   —in aching hearts.
There always is, in the presence of heavenly bodies,
a letting go of frustrations and tensions,
a drawing closer to the unknown.
And we were amazed
to discover
like those women at the Easter tomb
that there were angels
accompanying her on her journey
   —strong angels
   —unflagging angels
   —committed angels
holding her hand gently
taking her ever so slowly
   —so she wouldn't be afraid—
across the threshold of ambivalence
helping her set her course firmly
into the Angelic East
where Christ himself
and a cloud of loved ones
wait with arms outstretched
and sing with renewed and youthful voices:
Alleluia beautiful one!
Welcome pilgrim!
We've been waiting for you.

SECOND CHANCE (Easter, 2010)

You're here again.
Me too.
Some of us do this every year.
We gather to wait, to watch,
to vigil ourselves into Easter,
into another chance.
Words can't describe it.
It is hard to express
why we are here...
what we expect.
I am not one of those gifted writers
who can capture in a word
that shiver of sadness
that seizes your spine
and explodes through your body
when an anchor that held you fast
breaks loose and falls
to the bottom of life's ocean
leaving you to drift alone
with your thoughts.
I can't put that feeling into a few words.
No one can.
I am not one of those people
who can capture in a song
the soaring joy that comes
from newborn life,
giving a family hope for another generation.
Who can express that in a song?
I am not one of those people
who can describe in perfect syntax
the joys that lift us up,
the sorrows that weigh us down.
My words do not so much
convey thoughts but rather
convulse feelings,
haltingly.
Does that count?

I am not the one
who can tell you why you are here.

It is too intense
too complex
too overwhelming.
It occurs to me though,
that we are like people
waiting on a train platform
waiting for that train
that will take us someplace
we don't know
and can't describe
but desperately need to go.

I think that is why you are here.
I think that is why so many people
show up for Easter.
Some say they are just
Easter or Christmas Catholics.
And that may be true.
But I think it is something more.
I think all of us,
at a deeper level,
know we need another train,
know there is something more to us,
know we want another chance
to get it right.

There is a song.
It was written ten years ago.
I heard it for the first time this year.
It haunted me.
I don't know why for sure.
Again, I don't have the words.
　　　—Maybe it is because I am restless.
　　　—Maybe it is because my father was an old Railroad Man.
　　　—Maybe it is because I believe we all need to start over.
　　　—Maybe it is because it captured the words I don't have.
　　　—Maybe it is because it expresses a conviction about my own
　　　　life.
It touched me on many levels
because it is really about
Second Chances.
(I know about second chances.)

And as I prepared these Easter words
that song came crashing in on me again.

The refrain goes like this:
  "There's another train, there always is,
  Maybe the next one is yours,
  Get up and climb aboard another train."

We are like ALL the people
who have ever waited on a platform.
They were leaving somewhere
or heading somewhere.
They were running away
or going home.
Some even seemed to be going to die.
But all were moving to new life.
Really.

The first verse of that song says:
  "The beginning is now and will always be,
  You say you lost your chance and fate brought you defeat,
  But that means nothing. You look so sad,
  You've been listening to those who say you missed your
  chance."
But:
  "There's another train, there always is,
  Maybe the next one is yours,
  Get up and climb aboard another train."

Every Easter we gather on the platform
—not with luggage and suitcases and steamer trunks—
no, only with
Our Raging Fire
Our Springs of Water
Our Saving Oil
Our Life Giving Bread
Our Cup of Blessing.
It is all we need.
Resurrection and New Life
don't need any baggage.
Resurrection and New Life
are tricky
indescribable
beyond words.

Jesus couldn't tell his followers.
Maybe even he did not have the words.
They had to experience it
    —like touching your finger to a flame.
They had to feel it
    —like a wind blowing through your life.
They had to believe it
    —like a Man who knew he was dead.

Could this be your year?
Could this be your Easter?
Could this be your Second Chance?

    There's another train, there always is,
    Maybe the next one is yours,
    Get up and climb aboard another train...

(Song lyrics to "Another Train" by Pete Morton)

NOTHING SHOULD BE THE SAME (Christmas, 2010)

Once you have seen angels
flash across your sky...
Once you have allowed shepherds
to sleep on your hillside...
Once you have let wise men
cross your horizon...
Nothing should be the same.
Nothing can be boring or shallow.
Nothing can be interpreted
in the old economy of life.

Never then interpret the gentleness of a mother
as weakness.
It is rather a tender strength
born of fierce love
and a peaceful heart.

Never consider the faithfulness of a father
dispensable or guaranteed.
It is rather the rolling daily drumbeat
of a decision ever new and fresh
in the face of challenge failure and love.

Never interpret the tears
of a man of faith
as those watery children born of sadness.
No! They are always the overflowing
of a jubilant river
inside a heart
that has said YES
to the beauty of life
even when it beats within a chest
of doubt and fear.

Never think that the quiet smile
of a woman in love
is a passive acceptance
of all that is and was before.
That smile is the patient expectation
of more than dreams can promise
and of the fierce commitment
to change the world.

243

Now that Christ has been born
the closing door and the clenched fist,
the doubt and the dreariness,
the aging and the Alzheimer's,
the cancer and the cantankerousness,
the broken bones and the broken hearts
NEED NEVER DEFINE US!
Like Christmas itself
we can leap from the collective calendar
of our somber days
and anticipate
something golden and glowing.
We are a people redeemed,
sustained in an incarnational world.
We are children living life
in an outpouring of joy,
wrapped as if in a down comforter
of memories and hopes.

We are people who have walked
to where the sidewalk ends
and now must fly into the eternal East
to embrace a new Day
even as the midnight star
leaves its shimmering residue
on our beleaguered landscape.

Now we are haloed
by meridians of hope
interlacing us to the soaring universe
connecting us to the cosmic Christ
who has long since left
Bethlehem and baby-land
to be housed in the inn of our corporate heart
where loneliness overcome
    has helped us make a bed of revival and comfort...
where poverty undone
    has allowed us to set an expansive Table
    of nourishment and plenty...
where sickness embraced
    has taught us to breathe deeply the vibrant air of life...

where fear put in its place
    has set us free to open the door in anticipation and hope...
where imagination nurtured
    has hung the walls with frames of color and depth.
Do you recognize the place?
Open your eyes.
It is your home.
It is your heart.
It is your opportunity.

Here we hang on the edge of Christmas
Lighting candles
Baking bread
Pouring wine
Looking for the courage
to let ourselves fall
into the radiant stillness
of a magnificent love
beyond our wildest dreams.
Stop grasping. Stop clinging.
Let go.
Let go.

IF EASTER-PEOPLE ONLY KNEW (2011)

If Easter-people only knew.
We pass as pilgrims
to a place called Easter.
More than an idea or an ideology,
certainly more than a day,
Easter is a site located
within the very heart of God.
It is a holy place beyond geography.
If Easter-people only knew.
Pilgrims to other sites always return
with souvenirs and trinkets
and, if they are lucky, a memory.
I carried water back from Lourdes once,
before the day when holy water
posed an in-flight hazard to hapless
travelers in a terror ridden world.
Another time, I carried shells
from the coast of Maine.
The trunk of my car smelled
like a bad fish market on a hot day.
Then there was the time I smuggled seeds
from Calabria, thinking I could grow
memories of my father on fragile limbs.
We do what we can in a vaporous world.
The pilgrimage to Easter is different.
If Easter-people only knew.
We collect no souvenirs and
take no photographs.
But what we carry does pose a threat
to a world in the grip of
money, power, wealth and war.
If Easter-people only knew.
There is an explosive power in this pilgrimage.
We would never pass through
the unsubstantial security systems
of an idolatrous world.
The devil in all his disguises
knows that we could engulf the planet
in flames of love beyond imagination.
These flames could vaporize
hunger, loneliness, war and death.

If Easter-people only knew.
We are inflamed,
even when we travel
wet and shivering,
bundled up against a Springtime
that will not leave the cold cave of Winter.
When it seems that each day,
we look out water spotted windows
wondering when the rain will withdraw,
it is then that the flame sustains us.
Daffodils do bloom in the snow
and farmers will venture out
into once water logged fields to
sow the seeds of summer.
We carry the burning sun
even in leaden hearts.
If Easter-people only knew.

We are pilgrims into Easter.
Matthew tells us that when Jesus died
"The earth shook and the rocks were split."
Later he tells us the Daybreak
of that first Easter was shattered
with "a great earthquake."
What is his preoccupation with seismic shifts?
If Easter-people only knew.
Within each of us there is an Earthquake
of tectonic proportions that will bring,
not devastation, homelessness and nuclear disaster,
but a glorious shift in the very axis
of our spinning world.
A shift away from paralyzing fear.
A shift away from narrow thinking.
A shift away from old models of languid living.
If Easter-people only knew.
Our pilgrimage into Easter
does not allow us to remain at the tomb.
We build no monuments to death.
Jesus is not there, not contained.
He can never be merely enshrined
in churches, in tabernacles, in granite or stone.
No, he is unleashed, in love,
like a fire, like an explosion, like an earthquake.

If Easter-people only knew.
This is the legacy of our
Pilgrimage into Easter.
Jesus did not stay in the manger.
Jesus did not stay on the Cross.
Jesus did not stay in the grave.
Nor do we.
When we venture on that
Pilgrimage into Easter
We are inflamed.
We are earthquaked.
We rise.

If Easter-people only knew.

STRONG HEARTS

The Wind (of change)
blows against the Limits
of things (thought immovable)
and the Heart grows strong.
So sing a Song
for strong Hearts
secure in Love,
safe in a sheltered harbor
of friendship and fidelity.

NOTICING CHRISTMAS (2011)

Would I have noticed
the sudden
Whiteness
Brightness
Lightness
of that Holy Night
when it came in gentle
quiet explosion
into a world
dark and heavy
with sin and selfishness?
What is so different
between then and now?
Emperor Augustus has a new name.
But there are more than enough
tyrants, presidents and corporate giants
to go 'round.
Overwhelmed with political pessimism
I may overlook the opportunity
to travel home for a reunion,
preferring instead
to canonize my complaining.
Like the Befana of Italy
or the Babushka of Russia
so taken with the responsibilities of life
I leave no time for the Christ.

Gruff innkeepers still stand
behind commercial counters
hawking their wares,
refusing us service.
No surprise that Christ
is dismissed to the back barn.
The rich barter
their crowns, gifts and wisdom
for virtual reality.
How could they recognize a miracle?
The poor trade in
their crooks and staffs
for VCRs and superficial stuff.
How could they embrace another child?

Would I have noticed
the sudden
Whiteness
Brightness
Lightness
of that Holy Night?
Dull-witted and narrow,
slow to understand,
slower still to change our point of view,
we package the Christmas Mystery
like any other purchase,
with wrapping so elaborate
we miss the mystery.

Unwed mothers still give birth
and although the judgments are less
the care is not increased.
And just what are swaddling clothes?
There are no mangers to house them.
Dumpsters and abandoned cars
keep out the cold reality
of unfavorable winds.
And who would look for Christ
in such places?

Do Herald Angels
know that the fields near Bethlehem
have been supplanted
by freeways and malls?
Or are they like muddled Canada geese
looking for a bulldozed lake,
honking only to one another,
leaving us to our over-crowded underdevelopment?
Yet here in this wasteland
we would happily harken
to a Herald Angel or two.
But taking time is required.

Would I have noticed
the sudden
Whiteness
Brightness
Lightness?
It is a mystery.

We feebly endeavor to delve
with our sincere wishes,
our gift exchanges,
our holiday meals,
our remembering and reconciliations.
We are not evil people,
only diminished somehow.
But attitude never outlasts style.
Substance outweighs shallowness every time.
The truth bears the burden of the centuries
and rises once again
to confront us
with exactly what we need.

Would I have noticed?
So I reach out for a hand to hold.
A young hand (plump with new life)
clutching tenaciously to the hostile world.
An old hand
weak and weary and brittle
from which the flow of life
is slowly ebbing.
A working hand
calloused and bruised from toil
and who knows what.
A hungry hand
holding nothing but its own want.
A loyal hand
offering redemption
in the face of
hard-headedness and self-pity.

I take them all.
Or they take me.
And then I notice
the sudden
Whiteness
Brightness
Lightness
effused without restraint
in a murky world
where hidden only in the shadow I cast
the Christ has been waiting
all the while.

251

I STILL REMEMBER (August 10, 2014)

I still remember
the taste and silkiness
of the chocolate milk
gulped from the little glass bottle
that sat on the floor
next to the runner of my desk.
It was first grade
but I still remember.
And I remember too
the warmth and feel
of that first kiss
stolen from the little girl
with ringlets
who sat in the desk across the aisle.
(I remember her name!)
I remember that kiss.

And I remember
Mrs. Murphy
who looked more like someone's mother
than a real live schoolteacher.
She taught me my first Communion catechism
and proudly marshaled us down the aisle
on that First Communion Day
at nine o'clock Mass.
I still remember that day.
I remember, too,
the all white suit and shoes
the grass-stains on my knees
the changing, too late, into play clothes
so my cousins and I could
run to the creek
and play Tarzan across the rippling water.
I remember, at the end of the day,
opening all my cards
from aunts and uncles and godparents.
I remember counting fifty-two dollars
and thinking I was rich.
I remember all that.

And I remember
the sweet scent
of Sister Ursula's gabardine habit
of her hand lotion
as I sat on her lap
wondering if she could be the Blessed Mother herself.
I still remember.

I remember too
the taste of the stinging salty tears
that streamed down my face
when Sister Carmel
    —who I knew loved me more
    than she loved the Irish kids—
scolded me for missing
my early Mass serving day.

I remember
the flowing red cassocks
the starched white surplices
the crisp satin neck bows
the long silent processions
the sweet smell of incense and candlewax
the sound of the clicker
that magically made us kneel in unison
before mysteries we could not explain
even as they penetrated into our Catholic bones.

I remember clear as day
the swelling in my chest
after a mad flurry
of chalk dust and racing feet
when I got more points
than Mike Basile
for diagramming
the most complex, compound sentence
across the big blackboard
that spanned the front
of the 7th grade classroom.

And I remember
    that same year
    at the 7th grade party
    in Barbara Marco's basement
the sensation
when one of the girls
(I forget her name!)
plunged her tongue
into my mouth
during the non-stop kissing games
that 7th graders thought
would make them all grown up.

I remember the feeling
of lost innocence
of anticipation
of excitement
of fear
as I left the safety of
that grade school fortress
that had cradled me
and protected me
from the vicissitudes and vagaries of life
even before I knew
what those words meant.
I remember.
I remember.

THE GORGE (Urbino to Loreto, 2014)

Better than a photograph
my mind's eye even now sees

the gorge
and there is clarity.

Shimmering, still
glittering, rushing. It is all

and it is nothing. And
I am not looking

at it but am rather
in it.

Is the Italian sun
such a trickster or

am I so foolish
as to think this moment

could last forever and not know
that I too float

away on the current
away on the gorge air?

The refractions of my eye
careen off the sheer

stone walls, somersault across
the blading water

and come to rest
at my lumbering feet on the spot

where my DNA is now part
of the Marchegiana landscape.

MYSTERY WITHIN (Easter, 2015)

At first Jesus was not risen
only missing.
The three Marys didn't know about Resurrection.
He was just missing.
Missing.
I feel that way sometimes
don't you?
Missing. Out of touch. Insulated. Isolated.
Long lonely days
when resurrection is unknown,
maybe a wavering glimmer,
an aching hope, if that.
Sleepless nights
when life as we know it is MISSING,
when our only frame of reference is MISSING.

But then
from out of the black hole,
from out of the lurking tombs we build
there comes an ethereal angel...
An angel with a "Don't be discouraged."
"Don't be afraid."
"Don't be amazed."
But we are discouraged.
We are afraid.
And we can only hope to be amazed.
Mary Magdalene was probably the practical one,
worrying about who would roll away the obstinate stone.
She knew the three of them would be on their own.
Talk about missing!
They were all hiding out, the disciples!
But then, three women wouldn't draw much attention,
early in the morning,
doing women things.
Those men wouldn't have known what to do anyway.
So there she was, with the other Marys,
left alone, that stone to contend with.
It was a worry.
I get like that too, don't you?
Worrying about the stone,
worrying about the distracting details.

It is easier than dealing with death,
and life.
Turns out the stone was not the issue.
Isn't that always the case?
Fussing about details when something really big
is on the horizon.
Now this, an empty tomb!

They couldn't keep it to themselves.
They would have to tell the others,
at least Peter and John.
On the way, I wonder if the Magdalene began to hope,
began to figure it out.
I'll bet that's what happened.
In a heartbeat,
Resurrection began to settle quietly in her bones.
By the time she got to Peter and John,
there had to be something in her voice,
something in her look,
something beyond the words,
something she wasn't even conscious of,
something Peter sensed,
something John hoped for.
I can do that too.
So can you.
We can carry something within us,
something beyond consciousness,
something we are not even aware of,
something awesome and animated,
something that can inspire others.
It is like those times
when someone thanks you
for something you did or said
that came unwittingly
from some secret place within.
You don't know where.
I think that is what happened to Mary.
Peter and John didn't challenge her.
They knew better.
She was on to something,
something mysterious.
They had to go see,
they had to find out.

Isn't that why we are here?
To find out?
To discover? To see?
We come here with something missing.
We come looking for angels.
We come discouraged or afraid.
We come wanting to be amazed.
We come worrying about stones and details.
We come with gifts we didn't even know we had.
We come doing our best,
doing what we do,
just like the three Marys.
Maybe, like the Magdalene
we are on to something.
Maybe it is in us.
After all, real faith isn't just something we ever HAVE.
Real faith is something we always are growing into.
It is always something building within us,
just like in Mary.
So we come here today
to be confronted by
Fire
Word
Water
Sacrament
Sign & Symbol.
Are these strong enough
to bear the burden of faith?
Are these symbols powerful enough
to bear the burden
of all that we can be?
Are they big enough
to capture all the unknown mystery within us?
I think they are.
Let's give them a chance.

ANOTHER CHRISTMAS, NOW

One is tempted to say
life is changed
because of Christmas Day
    this Word made flesh
    this Virgin's child
    this Emmanuel
    this angeling and heralding
    this gift beyond measure.
But life is not merely changed or rearranged.
No.
Life is given.
Where before, on our own,
we were selfish, sinning, scheming
orphaned
helpless, homeless, hateful
dead.
Now we are
generous, forgiven, thoughtful
nurtured
strong, settled, loving,
alive!
The Baptist's cry
shattered our silence
and roused us
from a self-imposed sleep.
The prophets' promises
spoke to our longing
and caused that blood to course again
through collapsed veins.
The quiet "yes"
of a wide-eyed Jewish girl
wakened us to our own possibilities.
The strong faith
of a confused carpenter
has pulled us from the hopeless pit
we dug so diligently.

In the beginning was the Word
and the beginning is now, now, now.
The Word is now.

Now everything is different.
New.
Alive.
Unwed mother—now Blessed Mother.
Sleeping man—now Man of Dreams.
Homeless couple—now Sheltered Love.
Child of poverty—now Child of God.

But this life
this now
this opportunity
this new beginning
must be seized, grasped, treasured.
Or we will be reduced
again
to a death of
torn bows
shredded paper
forgotten cards
stale cookies.

The notes of the angels' song
can only be hung on the staff of our hearts
in full measure
so that when they return to heaven
we have left, on earth
all we need to live:
        the music of life
        the song to set us free.
Then, when fully alive
breathing deeply again
with no more shallow panting,
then, the possibilities are unbounded.
Every child becomes the Child.
Every woman is mother of the race.
Every man is Joseph-dreamer.

Infused with this illimitable life...
Disappointment is just that pesky test that comes before
        fulfillment.
Sickness is just that troublesome detour that precedes health.
Death is nothing more than a passing prelude to more life.

Yes, Christmas
one little day
can begin all this.
We know it.
We sense it.
We feel it.
Somewhere deep in the clan heart
troved into the culture
rooted in our collective memory
we know it is a day that is meant
to span into a lifetime.
Not just 24 hours, but infinity.
The family and friends and food
the laughter and tears
the memories and hopes
the prophecies and promises
the yeses and dreams
the Word made flesh
are all meant to be for every day.
We are never to be reduced to
a drive-by celebration
a fast-food existence.
We are meant for life.
And the gift
once given
will never be taken away.

EMBRACING THE DARKNESS (December, 2015)

I remember...when streetlights
weren't so bright.
They didn't turn night into day.
From rippled, hanging saucers
the bulbs cast white circles
on the pavement below.
It was better then.
You could run from white spot to white spot.
But if you liked,
you could hide in the dark spaces,
feeling safe,
knowing the light was close by.
Ironically, you could see the world
more clearly from the darkness
once your eyes and heart adjusted.

I remember...when mothers didn't need cell phones
to text you home.
A yell from the back door was more than enough.
It was better then.
When darkness fell
and it was time to go,
you could always linger for a moment or two,
comfortable in the shadows of dusk.
(She called it dawdling.)
You could look back on the freedom of the day
knowing that the morning light
would bring more of the same.

I remember...the big culvert in Lincoln Park.
We thought it was a tunnel
where spies and commies used to hide out.
I could stand up straight and run and jump
and not hit my head.
It was better then (before I was too big).
We could hide there
and when we weren't yelling for one another,
we could be quiet in the darkness
and never be afraid.
You knew your friends were close
even if you couldn't see them.

With pen knives and string
and other objects
pilfered from dad's workbench,
you would protect each other
and always make it to the light
at the other end.

Now the dark places in our lives
are of a different sort.
Maybe more scary, maybe not.
But from this darkness,
if you let it settle,
you can still see the world more clearly.
You can still linger for a moment
and feel the freedom of the day.
You can still hide and be quiet
knowing your friends are close.
So embrace the darkness
(or let it embrace you).
Look forward or backward,
it doesn't matter.
It all seems clearer
from the darkness
where God, the eternal light, is waiting.

THE HEART SAILS AND SINGS

The Heart aches
    to know
    to be known.
The Heart breaks
    through walls
    of separation and doubt.
The heart Sails and Sings
    like a captive bird
    set free at last
    only to return
        (willingly)
    to a perch as secure
    as any lover's arms.

EPILOGUE

LEGACY

The old man spoke
giving slow birth to words
like lines from a play.
His steely grey eyes
all the while
embracing the ones he loved.
His life
drifted beyond their reach.
His love
took hold of their hearts.
Even the young ones knew
the legacy he left behind
as he reminded them
that love is mostly memories.
And he had more than enough
(love)
to carry him safely
to the other side
while leaving them
more than a happy ending.

ABOUT THE AUTHOR

Father Joseph Angelo Fata was a priest in the Diocese of Youngstown for 48 years, serving as Pastor of St. Luke Parish (Boardman) for 28 of those years. He also served as Pastor of St. Joseph Parish (Mantua), and Associate Pastor of Our Lady of Peace (Canton) and St. Aloysius (East Liverpool). He was a founding member of the social justice organization ACTION (Alliance for Congregational Transformation Influencing Our Neighborhoods).

A collection of his homilies, "From Mass to Mission," was published in 2015. He died on August 1, 2016 at the age of 74 after a long battle with cancer.

TOPICAL INDEX

SPECIAL PLACES